Fashion, Costume, and Culture

Clothing, Headwear, Body Decorations, and Footwear through the Ages

Fashion, Costume, *and* Culture

Clothing, Headwear, Body Decorations, and Footwear through the Ages

Volume 1:
The Ancient World

SARA PENDERGAST AND TOM PENDERGAST

SARAH HERMSEN, *Project Editor*

Detroit • New York • San Diego • San Francisco • Cleveland • New Haven, Conn. • Waterville, Maine • London • Munich

THOMSON

★ ™

GALE

Fashion, Costume, and Culture: Clothing, Headwear, Body Decorations, and Footwear through the Ages

Sara Pendergast and Tom Pendergast

Project Editor
Sarah Hermsen

Imaging and Multimedia
Dean Dauphinais, Dave Oblender

Composition
Evi Seoud

Editorial
Lawrence W. Baker

Product Design
Kate Scheible

Manufacturing
Rita Wimberley

Permissions
Shalice Shah-Caldwell, Ann Taylor

LIBRARY OF CONGRESS CATALOGING-IN-PUBLICATION DATA

Pendergast, Sara.
Fashion, costume, and culture: clothing, headwear, body decorations, and footwear through the ages / Sara Pendergast and Tom Pendergast; Sarah Hermsen, editor.
    p. cm.
Includes bibliographical references and index.
ISBN 0-7876-5417-5 (set hardcover)—ISBN 0-7876-5418-3 (v.1 : alk. paper)—
ISBN 0-7876-5419-1 (v.2 : alk. paper)—ISBN 0-7876-5420-5 (v.3 : alk. paper)—
ISBN 0-7876-5421-3 (v.4 : alk. paper)— ISBN 0-7876-5422-1 (v.5 : alk. paper)
1. Costume—History. 2. Fashion—History. 3. Body marking—History. 4. Dress accessories—History. I. Title: Clothing, headwear, body decorations, and footwear through the ages. II. Pendergast, Tom. III. Hermsen, Sarah. IV. Title. GT511.P46 2004
391'.009—dc22
                                          2003015852

Printed in the United States of America
10 9 8 7 6 5 4 3 2 1

Contents

■ ■ ■

■
■
■ *Volume 1:* The Ancient World
■

PREHISTORY

ANCIENT EGYPT

Volume 2: Early Cultures Across the Globe

EARLY ASIAN CULTURES

AFRICAN CULTURES

■
■
■ *Volume 3:* European Culture from
■   the Renaissance to the Modern Era

THE FIFTEENTH CENTURY

THE SIXTEENTH CENTURY

∎
∎
∎
∎ *Volume 4:* Modern World
   Part I: 1900 to 1945

1900–18

Volume 5: Modern World
Part II: 1946 to 2003

Clothing

Headwear

Body Decorations

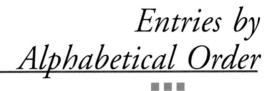

Entries by Alphabetical Order

A

B

▌ C ▌

D

E

F

G

H

I

J

‖ K

‖ L

‖ M

‖ N

O

P

R

S

‖ T

‖ U

‖ V

‖ W

Z

Entries by Topic Category

∎∎∎

‖ Clothing

▌ Headwear

▌ Body Decorations

▌ Footwear

Reader's Guide

■ ■ ■

Fashion, Costume, and Culture: Clothing, Headwear, Body Decorations, and Footwear through the Ages provides a broad overview of costume traditions of diverse cultures from prehistoric times to the present day. The five-volume set explores various items of human decoration and adornment, ranging from togas to turbans, necklaces to tennis shoes, and discusses why and how they were created, the people who made them, and their uses. More than just a description of what people wore and why, this set also describes how clothing, headwear, body decorations, and footwear reflect different cultural, religious, and societal beliefs.

Volume 1 covers the ancient world, including prehistoric man and the ancient cultures of Egypt, Mesopotamia, India, Greece, and Rome. Key issues covered in this volume include the early use of animal skins as garments, the introduction of fabric as the primary human body covering, and the development of distinct cultural traditions for draped and fitted garments.

Volume 2 looks at the transition from the ancient world to the Middle Ages, focusing on the Asian cultures of China and Japan, the Byzantine Empire, the nomadic and barbarian cultures of early Europe, and Europe in the formative Middle Ages. This volume also highlights several of the ancient cultures of North America, South and Central America, and Africa that were encountered by

Europeans during the Age of Exploration that began in the fifteenth century.

Volumes 3 through 5 offer chronological coverage of the development of costume and fashion in the West. Volume 3 features the costume traditions of the developing European nation-states in the fifteenth through the nineteenth centuries, and looks at the importance of the royal courts in introducing clothing styles and the shift from home-based garmentmaking to shop-based and then factory-based industry.

Volumes 4 and 5 cover the period of Western history since 1900. These volumes trace the rise of the fashion designer as the primary creator of new clothing styles, chart the impact of technology on costume traditions, and present the innovations made possible by the introduction of new synthetic, or man-made, materials. Perhaps most importantly, Volumes 4 and 5 discuss what is sometimes referred to as the democratization of fashion. At the beginning of the twentieth century, high quality, stylish clothes were designed by and made available to a privileged elite; by the middle to end of the century, well-made clothes were widely available in the West, and new styles came from creative and usually youth-oriented cultural groups as often as they did from designers.

Organization

Fashion, Costume, and Culture is organized into twenty-five chapters, focusing on specific cultural traditions or on a specific chronological period in history. Each of these chapters share the following components:

- A chapter introduction, which discusses the general historical framework for the chapter and highlights the major social and economic factors that relate to the development of costume traditions.

- Four sections that cover Clothing, Headwear, Body Decorations, and Footwear. Each of these sections opens with an overview that discusses general trends within the broader category, and nearly every section contains one or more essays on specific garments or trends that were important during the period.

Each chapter introduction and individual essay in *Fashion, Costume, and Culture* includes a For More Information section listing sources—books, articles, and Web sites—containing additional information on fashion and the people and events it addresses. Some essays also contain *See also* references that direct the reader to other essays within the set that can offer more information on this or related items.

Bringing the text to life are more than 330 color or black-and-white photos and maps, while numerous sidebar boxes offer additional insight into the people, places, and happenings that influenced fashion throughout the years. Other features include tables of contents listing the contents of all five volumes, listing the entries by alphabetical order, and listing entries by category. Rounding out the set are a timeline of important events in fashion history, a words to know section defining terms used throughout the set, a bibliography of general fashion sources, including notable Web sites, and a comprehensive subject index, which provides easy access to the subjects discussed throughout *Fashion, Costume, and Culture.*

Acknowledgments

Many thanks to the following advisors who provided valuable comments and suggestions for *Fashion, Costume, and Culture:* Ginny Chaussee, Retired Media Specialist, Mountain Pointe High School, Phoenix, Arizona; Carol Keeler, Media Specialist, Detroit Country Day Upper School, Beverly Hills, Michigan; Nina Levine, Library Media Specialist, Blue Mountain Middle School, Cortlandt Manor, New York; and Bonnie Raasch, Media Specialist, C. B. Vernon Middle School, Marion, Iowa.

No work of this size could be completed without the efforts of many dedicated people. The authors would like to thank Sarah Hermsen, who shouldered the work of picture selection and ushered the book through copyediting and production. She deserves a good share of the credit for the success of this project. We also owe a great deal to the writers who have helped us create the hundreds of essays in this book: Tina Gianoulis, Rob Edelman, Bob Schnakenberg, Audrey Kupferberg, and Carol Brennan. The staff at U•X•L has been a pleasure to work with, and Carol Nagel and Tom Romig deserve special mention for the cheerfulness and professionalism they bring to their work. We'd also like to thank the staffs of two libraries, at the University of Washington and the Sno-Isle Regional Library, for allowing us to ransack and hold hostage their costume collections for months at a time.

We cannot help but mention the great debt we owe to the costume historians whose works we have consulted, and whose names appear again and again in the bibliographies of the essays. We sincerely hope that this collection pays tribute to and furthers their collective production of knowledge.

—Sara Pendergast and Tom Pendergast

Comments and Suggestions

We welcome your comments on *Fashion, Costume, and Culture* as well as your suggestions for topics to be featured in future editions. Please write to: Editor, *Fashion, Costume, and Culture,* U•X•L, 27500 Drake Road, Farmington Hills, Michigan, 48331-3535; call toll-free: 800-877-4253; fax to 248-414-5043; or send e-mail via http://www.gale.com.

Contributors

■■■

CAROL BRENNAN. Freelance Writer, Grosse Pointe, MI.

ROB EDELMAN. Instructor, State University of New York at Albany. Author, *Baseball on the Web* (1997) and *The Great Baseball Films* (1994). Co-author, *Matthau: A Life* (2002); *Meet the Mertzes* (1999); and *Angela Lansbury: A Life on Stage and Screen* (1996). Contributing editor, *Leonard Maltin's Move & Video Guide, Leonard Maltin's Movie Encyclopedia,* and *Leonard Maltin's Family Viewing Guide.* Contributing writer, *International Dictionary of Films and Filmmakers* (2000); *St. James Encyclopedia of Popular Culture* (2000); *Women Filmmakers & Their Films* (1998); *The Political Companion to American Film* (1994); and *Total Baseball* (1989). Film commentator, WAMC (Northeast) Public Radio.

TINA GIANOULIS. Freelance Writer. Contributing writer, *World War I Reference Library* (2002); *Constitutional Amendments: From Freedom of Speech to Flag Burning* (2001); *International Dictionary of Films and Filmmakers* (2000); *St. James Encyclopedia of Popular Culture* (2000); and mystories.com, a daytime drama Web site (1997–98).

AUDREY KUPFERBERG. Film consultant and archivist. Instructor, State University of New York at Albany. Co-author, *Matthau: A Life* (2002); *Meet the Mertzes* (1999); and *Angela Lansbury: A Life on Stage and Screen* (1996). Contributing editor, *Leonard Maltin's*

Family Viewing Guide. Contributing writer, *St. James Encyclopedia of Popular Culture* (2000). Editor, *Rhythm* (2001), a magazine of world music and global culture.

SARA PENDERGAST. President, Full Circle Editorial. Vice president, Group 3 Editorial. Co-editor, *St. James Encyclopedia of Popular Culture* (2000). Co-author, *World War I Reference Library* (2002), among other publications.

TOM PENDERGAST. Editorial director, Full Circle Editorial. Ph.D., American studies, Purdue University. Author, *Creating the Modern Man: American Magazines and Consumer Culture* (2000). Co-editor, *St. James Encyclopedia of Popular Culture* (2000).

ROBERT E. SCHNAKENBERG. Senior writer, History Book Club. Author, *The Encyclopedia Shatnerica* (1998).

Timeline

■ ■ ■

THE BEGINNING OF HUMAN LIFE ■ Early humans wrap themselves in animal hides for warmth.

c. 10,000 B.C.E. ■ Tattooing is practiced on the Japanese islands, in the Jomon period (c. 10,000–300 B.C.E.). Similarly scarification, the art of carving designs into the skin, has been practiced since ancient times in Oceania and Africa to make a person's body more beautiful or signify a person's rank in society.

c. 3100 B.C.E. ■ Egyptians weave a plant called flax into a light cloth called linen and made dresses and loincloths from it.

c. 3100 B.C.E. ■ Egyptians shave their heads to keep themselves clean and cool in the desert heat, but covered their heads with wigs of various styles.

c. 10,000 B.C.E.
Humans populated most of
the major landmasses
on Earth

■

c. 7000 B.C.E.
The first human settlements
were developed in
Mesopotamia

■

10,000 B.C.E.

7000 B.C.E.

c. 3100 B.C.E. ■ Egyptians perfume their bodies by coating their skin in fragrant oils and ointments.

c. 3000 B.C.E. ■ Men and women in the Middle East, Africa, and the Far East have wrapped turbans on their heads since ancient times, and the turban continues to be popular with both men and women in many modern cultures.

c. 2600 B.C.E. TO 900 C.E. ■ Ancient Mayans, whose civilization flourishes in Belize and on the Yucatan Peninsula in Mexico, flatten the heads of the children of wealthy and powerful members of society. The children's heads are squeezed between two boards to elongate their skulls into a shape that looks very similar to an ear of corn.

c. 2500 B.C.E. ■ Indians wear a wrapped style of trousers called a dhoti and a skirt-like lower body covering called a lungi.

c. 2500 B.C.E. ■ Indian women begin to adorn themselves in the wrapped dress style called a sari.

c. 1500 B.C.E. ■ Egyptian men adopt the tunic as an upper body covering when Egypt conquers Syria.

c. 27 B.C.E.–476 C.E. ■ Roman soldiers, especially horsemen, adopt the trousers, or feminalia, of the nomadic tribes they encounter on the outskirts of the Roman Empire.

SIXTH AND FIFTH CENTURIES B.C.E. ■ The doric chiton becomes one of the most popular garments for both men and women in ancient Greece.

FIFTH CENTURY B.C.E. ■ The toga, a wrapped garment, is favored by Romans.

c. 3500 B.C.E. Beginnings of Sumerian civilization	c. 2680–2526 B.C.E. Building of the Great Pyramids near Giza, Egypt	c. 1792–1750 B.C.E. Hammurabi creates empire of Babylonia	44 B.C.E. Julius Caesar becomes Roman dictator for life and is then assassinated
■	■	■	■
4000 B.C.E.	**3000 B.C.E.**	**2000 B.C.E.**	**1000 B.C.E.**

c. 476 ■ Upper-class men, and sometimes women, in the Byzantine Empire (476–1453 C.E.) wear a long, flowing robe-like overgarment called a dalmatica developed from the tunic.

c. 900 ■ Young Chinese girls tightly bind their feet to keep them small, a sign of beauty for a time in Chinese culture. The practice was outlawed in 1911.

c. 1100–1500 ■ The cote, a long robe worn by both men and women, and its descendant, the cotehardie, are among the most common garments of the late Middle Ages.

1392 ■ Kimonos are first worn in China as an undergarment. The word "kimono" later came to be used to describe the native dress of Japan in the nineteenth century.

MIDDLE AGES ■ Hose and breeches, which cover the legs individually, become more common garments for men.

FOURTEENTH CENTURY TO SIXTEENTH CENTURY ■ Cuts and openings in garments made from slashing and dagging decorate garments from upper body coverings to shoes.

1470 ■ The first farthingales, or hoops worn under a skirt to hold it out away from the body, are worn in Spain and are called vertugados. These farthingales become popular in France and England and are later known as the Spanish farthingale.

FIFTEENTH CENTURY AND SIXTEENTH CENTURY ■ The doublet—a slightly padded short overshirt, usually buttoned down the front, with or without sleeves—becomes an essential men's garment.

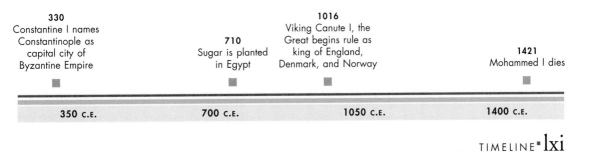

330
Constantine I names
Constantinople as
capital city of
Byzantine Empire
■

710
Sugar is planted
in Egypt
■

1016
Viking Canute I, the
Great begins rule as
king of England,
Denmark, and Norway
■

1421
Mohammed I dies
■

| 350 C.E. | 700 C.E. | 1050 C.E. | 1400 C.E. |

LATE FIFTEENTH THROUGH THE SIXTEENTH CENTURY ■ The ruff, a wide pleated collar, often stiffened with starch or wire, is worn by wealthy men and women of the time.

SIXTEENTH CENTURY ■ Worn underneath clothing, corsets squeeze and mold women's bodies into the correct shape to fit changing fashions of dress.

SIXTEENTH CENTURY ■ People carry or wear small pieces of animal fur in hopes that biting fleas will be more attracted to the animal's skin than to their own.

LATE MIDDLE AGES ■ The beret, a soft, brimless wool hat, is the most popular men's hat during the late Middle Ages and into the fifteenth and sixteenth centuries, especially in France, Italy, and Spain.

1595 ■ Europeans land on the Marquesas Islands in Oceania and discover native inhabitants covered in tattoos.

SEVENTEENTH CENTURY ■ The Kuba people, living in the present-day nation of the Democratic Republic of the Congo, weave a decorative cloth called Kuba cloth. An entire social group of men and women is involved in the production of the cloth, from gathering the fibers, weaving the cloth, and dyeing the decorative strands, to applying the embroidery, appliqué, or patchwork.

SEVENTEENTH CENTURY ■ Canes become carefully crafted items and are carried by most well-dressed gentleman.

1643 ■ French courtiers begin wearing wigs to copy the long curly hair of the sixteen-year-old king, Louis XIV. The fashion for long wigs continues later when, at the age of thirty-five, Louis begins to cover his thinning hair with wigs to maintain his beloved style.

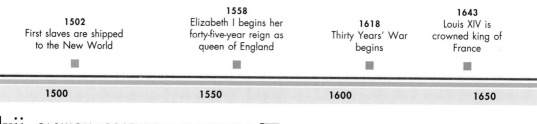

1502	1558	1618	1643
First slaves are shipped to the New World	Elizabeth I begins her forty-five-year reign as queen of England	Thirty Years' War begins	Louis XIV is crowned king of France
■	■	■	■

| 1500 | 1550 | 1600 | 1650 |

EIGHTEENTH CENTURY ■ French men tuck flowers in the buttonholes of their waistcoats and introduce boutonières as fashionable nosegays for men.

EIGHTEENTH CENTURY ■ The French Revolution (1789–99) destroys the French monarchy and makes ankle-length trousers fashionable attire for all men. Trousers come to symbolize the ideas of the Revolution, an effort to make French people more equal, and soon men of all classes are wearing long trousers.

1778 ■ À la Belle Poule, a huge hairstyle commemorating the victory of a French ship over an English ship in 1778, features an enormous pile of curled and powdered hair stretched over a frame affixed to the top of a woman's head. The hair is decorated with a model of the ship in full sail.

1849 ■ Dark blue, heavy-duty cotton pants—known as blue jeans—are created as work pants for the gold miners of the 1849 California gold rush.

1868 ■ A sturdy canvas and rubber shoe called a croquet sandal is introduced and sells for six dollars a pair, making it too expensive for all but the very wealthy. The shoe later became known as the tennis shoe.

1870 ■ A French hairstylist named Marcel Grateau invents the first long-lasting hair waving technique using a heated iron to give hair curls that lasts for days.

LATE 1800s TO EARLY 1900s ■ The feathered war bonnet, traditional to only a small number of Native American tribes, becomes known as a typical Native American headdress with the help of Buffalo Bill Cody's Wild West Show, which features theatrical representations of the Indians and cowboys of the American West and travels throughout America and parts of Europe.

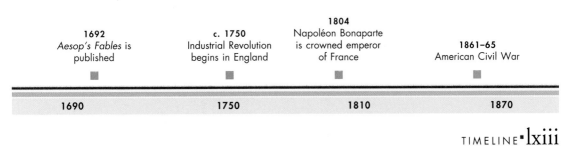

1692 Aesop's Fables is published	c. 1750 Industrial Revolution begins in England	1804 Napoléon Bonaparte is crowned emperor of France	1861–65 American Civil War
■	■	■	■
1690	1750	1810	1870

1900s ■ Loose, floppy, two-legged undergarments for women, bloomers start a trend toward less restrictive clothing for women, including clothing that allows them to ride bicycles, play tennis, and to take part in other sport activities.

1915 ■ American inventor T.L. Williams develops a cake of mascara and a brush to darken the lashes and sells them through the mail under the name Maybelline.

1920s ■ Advances in paint technology allow the creation of a hard durable paint and fuel an increase in the popularity of colored polish for fingernails and toenails.

1920s ■ The navy blue blazer, a jacket with brass buttons, becomes popular for men to wear at sporting events.

1920s ■ A fad among women for wearing short, bobbed hairstyles sweeps America and Europe.

1930s ■ Popular as a shirt for tennis, golf, and other sport activities for decades, the polo shirt becomes the most popular leisure shirt for men.

1939 ■ For the first time, *Vogue,* the respected fashion magazine, pictures women in trousers.

1945 ■ Servicemen returning home from World War II (1939–45) continue to wear the T-shirts they had been issued as undershirts during the war and soon the T-shirt becomes an acceptable casual outershirt.

1946 ■ The bikini, a two-piece bathing suit, is developed and named after a group of coral islands in the Pacific Ocean.

1950s ■ The gray flannel suit becomes the most common outfit worn by men working at desk jobs in office buildings.

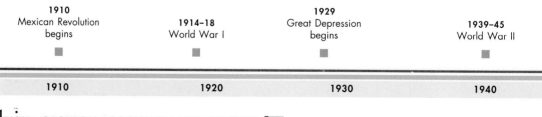

1910 Mexican Revolution begins	1914–18 World War I	1929 Great Depression begins	1939–45 World War II
■	■	■	■
1910	1920	1930	1940

1957 ■ Liquid mascara is sold at retail stores in tubes with a brush inside.

1960s AND 1970s ■ The afro, featuring a person's naturally curly hair trimmed in a full, evenly round shape around the head, is the most popular hairstyle among African Americans.

c. 1965 ■ Women begin wearing miniskirts with hemlines hitting at mid-thigh or above.

1980s ■ Power dressing becomes a trend toward wearing expensive, designer clothing for work.

1990s ■ Casual Fridays becomes the name given to the practice of allowing employees to dress informally on the last day of the work week.

1990s ■ Grunge, a trend for wearing old, sometimes stained or ripped clothing, becomes a fashion sensation and prompts designers to sell simple flannel shirts for prices in excess of one thousand dollars.

2000s ■ Versions of clothing available during the 1960s and 1970s, such as bell-bottom jeans and the peasant look, return to fashion as "retro fashions."

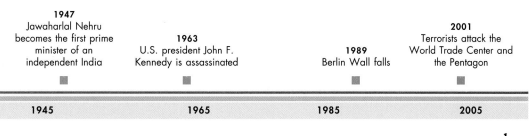

1947 Jawaharlal Nehru becomes the first prime minister of an independent India		**1963** U.S. president John F. Kennedy is assassinated		**1989** Berlin Wall falls	**2001** Terrorists attack the World Trade Center and the Pentagon	
■		■		■	■	
1945		**1965**		**1985**	**2005**	

Words to Know

■ ■ ■

▌ A

Appliqué: An ornament sewn, embroidered, or glued onto a garment.

▌ B

Bias cut: A fabric cut diagonally across the weave to create a softly draped garment.

Bodice: The part of a woman's garment that covers her torso from neck to waist.

Bombast: Padding used to increase the width or add bulk to the general silhouette of a garment.

Brim: The edge of a hat that projects outward away from the head.

Brocade: A fabric woven with a raised pattern over the entire surface.

C

Collar: The part of a shirt that surrounds the neck.

Crown: The portion of a hat that covers the top of the head; may also refer to the top part of the head.

Cuff: A piece of fabric sewn at the bottom of a sleeve.

D

Double-breasted: A style of jacket in which one side (usually the left) overlaps in the front of the other side, fastens at the waist with a vertical row of buttons, and has another row of buttons on the opposite side that is purely decorative. *See also* Single-breasted.

E

Embroidery: Needlework designs on the surface of a fabric, added for decoration.

G

Garment: Any article of clothing.

H

Hemline: The bottom edge of a skirt, jacket, dress, or other garment.

Hide: The pelt of an animal with the fur intact.

I

Instep: The upper surface of the arched middle portion of the human foot in front of the ankle joint.

J

Jersey: A knitted fabric usually made of wool or cotton.

L

Lapel: One of the two flaps that extend down from the collar of a coat or jacket and fold back against the chest.

Lasts: The foot-shaped forms or molds that are used to give shape to shoes in the process of shoemaking.

Leather: The skin or hide of an animal cleaned and treated to soften it and preserve it from decay.

Linen: A fabric woven from the fibers of the flax plant. Linen was one of the first woven fabrics.

M

Mule: A shoe without a covering or strap around the heel of the foot.

Muslin: A thin cotton fabric.

P

Patent Leather: Leather varnished and buffed to a high shine.

Placket: A slit in a dress, blouse, or skirt.

Pleat: A decorative feature on a garment in which fabric has been doubled over, pressed, and stitched in place.

Q

Queue: A ponytail of hair gathered at the back of a wig with a band.

R

Ready-to-wear: Clothing manufactured in standard sizes and sold to customers without custom alterations.

S

Silhouette: The general shape or outline of the human body.

Single-breasted: A jacket fastened down the front with a single row of buttons. *See also* Double-breasted.

Sole: The bottom of a shoe, covering the bottom of the foot.

Straights: The forms, or lasts, used to make the soles of shoes without differentiating between the left and right feet.

Suede: Skin from a young goat, called kidskin or calfskin, buffed to a velvet-like finish.

Synthetic: A term used to describe chemically made fabrics, such as nylon, acrylic, polyester, and vinyl.

T

Taffeta: A shiny, smooth fabric woven of silk or other materials.

Textile: A cloth or fabric, especially when woven or knitted.

Throat: The opening of a shoe at the instep.

Twill: A fabric with a diagonal line pattern woven onto the surface.

U

Upper: The parts of a shoe above the sole.

V

Velvet: A fabric with a short, plush pile of silk, cotton, or other material.

W

Wig: A head covering worn to conceal the hair or to cover a bald head.

Fashion, Costume, and Culture

Clothing, Headwear, Body Decorations, and Footwear through the Ages

Prehistoric Life

Scientists believe that the earliest stages of human evolution began in Africa about seven million years ago as a population of African apes evolved into three different species: gorillas, chimpanzees, and humans. Some three million years later early humans stood nearly upright and had developed larger brains, about half the size of the modern brain. By 2.5 million years ago it appears that these protohumans, as early humans are known, began to use crude tools such as chipped stones. Beginning about one million years ago, early humans began to migrate out of Africa and into other parts of the world. In a process that appears to have been completed around 10,000 B.C.E., humans spread throughout the world, populating most of the major landmasses of the earth.

As evolution continued man became taller and more intelligent and capable. He evolved from the species *Australopithecus* into *Homo habilis* into *Homo erectus* and finally, about 500,000 years ago, into the direct ancestors of modern man, *Homo sapiens*. Yet human development was not done. Neanderthal man, an early subspecies of *Homo sapiens* in human evolution, survived from about 200,000 years ago to about 30,000 years ago. Neanderthal man developed in several areas of the world and began to use more tools to hunt, to build shelters, and to develop the first known forms of human clothing. Evidence of Neanderthal man's existence has been found in Europe and in parts of Africa and the Middle East, but it is clear that the population was fairly small and not spread around the world.

Cro-Magnon man

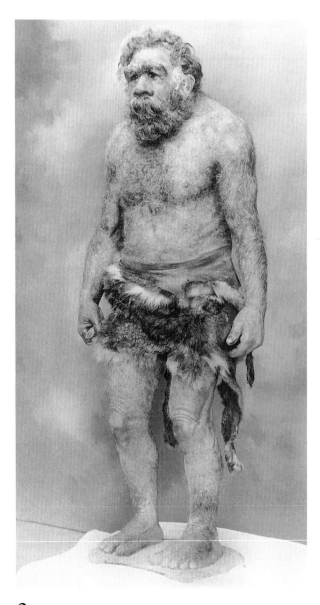

Cavepeople often wore loincloths made of animal skin. *Reproduced by permission of © Bettmann/ CORBIS.*

Overlapping somewhat with Neanderthal man was the sub-species from which modern man is directly descended, *Homo sapiens sapiens,* better known as Cro-Magnon man. Cro-Magnon man first began to appear around forty thousand years ago in various parts of the world, as far apart as Borneo, in Malaysia, and Europe. At first Cro-Magnon man was much like Neanderthal man in his use of tools, his methods of hunting and gathering food, and his creation of rough forms of clothing. But there were important physical differences between the subspecies. Cro-Magnon man stood fully upright, had a larger brain, a thinner nose, a more pronounced chin, and a skeletal structure nearly identical to modern man. Before too long, and for reasons that still puzzle scientists, the capabilities of Cro-Magnon man developed dramatically in what some call the "Great Leap Forward." Cro-Magnon man spread throughout the world, displacing Neanderthal man, who soon died out, and began to establish more elaborate groupings that soon developed into the first recognized permanent human settlements.

Cro-Magnon humans were largely hunter-gatherers, which meant their food depended on the animals that they killed and the fruits and plants they gathered from within their local surroundings. Hunter-gatherers were usually nomadic, moving from place to place as they exhausted the local food supply or following herds of deer, bison, or other prey. Because they had to move frequently, they kept their population low, so that they wouldn't have to transport many small children, and their clans small, so they wouldn't have too many people to feed. Over time they developed more sophisticated ways of making stone tools, such as arrow points and axes, and they also developed tools from the bones of animals. Because they lived in a climate that was much colder than the present climate (during this time the earth's temperature rose and fell dramatically, creating a series of ice ages), they needed to find ways to keep warm and dry. Animal skins provided their first forms of clothing and footwear, and Cro-Magnon man used tools such as rock and bone scrapers to strip the flesh and fat from the skins and cut the skins into primitive forms of clothing. In addition to making clothing, Cro-Magnon man began to decorate the human body with body paint and perhaps tattoos.

As the climate warmed and the human population grew and spread geographically, humans began to develop the first "civilized" human settlements, starting to grow their own food, to domesticate animals, and to live in permanent settlements. The first such settlements were developed as early as 7000 B.C.E. in the broad region known as Mesopotamia, centered in present-day Iraq near the Tigris and Euphrates Rivers. Mesopotamians, as those who lived in the area are referred to, developed the ability to create pottery from clay, learned to gather and spin wool from the sheep and goats that they herded, and developed systems of trade that soon expanded throughout the Middle East and into Europe and Asia. It was in Mesopotamia and the other great early civilization, Egypt, where clothing other than animal skins first began to be made and worn. Yet more primitive hunter-gatherer cultures continued to exist in many parts of the world well after the formation of the first civilizations, and indeed up to the modern day. These groups continued to rely on animal skins to provide their clothing.

How do we know?

The task of understanding the nature of early human life is very difficult. Scientists who study the material remains of past cultures, such as fossils, rocks, and human bones, are known as archeologists. They must use a very limited number of clues to reconstruct the nature of past human life. The older the human remains, the more difficult their work becomes. Years of burial beneath tons of earth and years of erosion and wear help to scatter and destroy evidence. Archeologists must carefully dig the remnants of the human past from out of the earth. They must form a picture of the whole based upon a very small part, guessing what a one-thousand-piece puzzle will look like after just fifty pieces.

Much of what archeologists know about past human life is uncertain and partial. For example, archeologists argue about the dates that human life began and changed. New discoveries constantly force scientists to rethink the dating given to major developments in human prehistory. Even the primary method of identifying the age of discoveries, known as radiocarbon dating, is subject to second-guessing. Often different sources have different dates. Another difficulty is that there are simply not many sources of evidence about early human life. Archeologists must form their picture of early life based on small sets of discovered materials separated by both time and distance. Because of these difficulties, much of what is known about prehistoric man is based on the best guesses of scientists who may have devoted their life's work to the subject.

The problem of understanding the clothing of early humans is made even more difficult by the fragile and destructible nature of fur. While bones and stones may survive for thousands of years, fur decomposes and disappears. The same is true with human hair and skin. But these difficulties do not mean we know nothing of early clothing and decoration. In some cases, human remains have been embedded in ice or discovered in extremely dry caves, and clothing has been preserved. Another form of evidence comes from early rock paintings and etchings that have depicted human clothes, hair, and body decoration. Though our knowledge of early clothing is minimal, we can get some picture of how our earliest ancestors protected themselves from the cold and, perhaps, made themselves beautiful or scary to their peers.

FOR MORE INFORMATION

Corbishley, Mike. *What Do We Know about Prehistoric People?* New York: Peter Bedrick Books, 1994.

Goode, Ruth. *People of the Ice Age.* New York: Crowell-Collier Press, 1973.

Hawkes, Jacquetta. *The Atlas of Early Man.* New York: St. Martin's Press, 1976.

Lambert, David, and the Diagram Group. *The Field Guide to Early Man.* New York: Facts on File, 1987.

Wilkinson, Phil, and Nick Merriman, eds. *Early Humans.* New York: Dorling Kindersley, 2000.

Prehistoric Clothing

The first known humans to make clothing, Neanderthal man, survived from about 200,000 B.C.E. to about 30,000 B.C.E. During this time the earth's temperature rose and fell dramatically, creating a series of ice ages throughout the northern areas of Europe and Asia where Neanderthal man lived. With their compact, muscular bodies that conserved body heat, Neanderthals were well adapted to the cold climate of their day. But it was their large brain that served them best. Neanderthal man learned to make crude but effective tools from stone. Tools such as spears and axes made Neanderthals strong hunters, and they hunted the hairy mammoths, bears, deer, musk oxen, and other mammals that shared their environment. At some point, Neanderthals learned how to use the thick, furry hides from these animals to keep themselves warm and dry. With this discovery, clothing was born.

Evidence of the very first clothing is mostly indirect. Archeologists (scientists who study the fossil and material remnants of past life) discovered chipped rock scrapers that they believe were used to scrape meat from animal hides. These date to about 100,000 B.C.E. Archeologists believe that these early humans cut the hides into shapes they liked, making holes for the head and perhaps the arms, and draped the furs over their bodies. Soon their methods likely grew more sophisticated. They may have used thin strips of hide to tie the furs about themselves, perhaps in the way that belts are used today.

Cro-Magnon man, considered the next stage in human development, emerged around forty thousand years ago and made advances in the clothing of the Neanderthals. The smarter Cro-Magnon people learned how to make fire and cook food, and they developed finer, more efficient tools. Sharp awls, or pointed tools, were used to punch small holes in animal skins, which were laced

This cave painting depicts the slaughter of an animal whose skin would be used for clothing and whose meat would be used for food. *Reproduced by permission of © Francis G. Mayer/CORBIS.*

together with hide string. In this way they probably developed the earliest coverings for the body, legs, head, and feet. It is thought that the first assembled piece of clothing was the tunic. A tunic is made from two pieces of rectangular animal hide bound together on one short side with a hole left for the head. This rough garment was placed over the head and the stitched length lay on the shoulders, with the remainder hanging down. The arms stuck through the open sides, and the garment was either closed with a belt or additional ties were placed at the sides to hold the garment on the body. This tunic was the ancestor of the shirt.

One of the most important Cro-Magnon inventions was the needle. Needles were made out of slivers of animal bone; they were sharpened to a point at one end and had an eye at the other end. With a needle, Cro-Magnon man could sew carefully cut pieces of fur into better fitting garments. Evidence suggests that Cro-Magnon people developed close-fitting pants and shirts that would protect them from the cold, as well as shawls, hoods, and long boots. Because they had not learned how to tan hides to soften them, the animal skin would have been stiff at first, but with repeated wearings it would become very soft and comfortable. Jacquetta Hawkes, author of *The Atlas of Early Man,* believes that Cro-Magnon clothes approached those of modern Eskimos in their excellence of construction.

Much of what is known about early clothing is a patchwork of very little evidence and good guesses. Only fragments of very early clothing have survived, so archeologists have relied on cave drawings, carved figures, and such things as the imprint of stitched-together skins in a fossilized mud floor to develop their picture of early clothing. The discovery of the remains of a man who died 5,300 years ago in the mountains of Austria, near the border with Italy, helped confirm much of what these archeologists had discovered. The body of this male hunter had been preserved in ice for over five thousand years, and many fragments of his clothing had survived.

Archeologists pieced together his garments, and they found that the iceman, as he became known, wore a complex outfit. Carefully sewn leggings covered his lower legs, and a thin leather loincloth was wrapped around his genitals and buttocks. Over his body the man wore a long-sleeved fur coat that extended nearly to his knees. The coat was sewn from many pieces of fur, with the fur on the outside. It was likely held close by some form of belt. On his feet the man wore animal hide short boots, stitched together with hide and stuffed with grass, probably to keep his feet warm in the snow. On his head the man wore a simple cap of thick fur. Though the iceman discovered in Austria appeared much later than the earliest Cro-Magnon man, the way his clothing was made confirmed the basic techniques and materials of early clothing. The ravages of time have destroyed most direct evidence of the clothing of early man, however.

FOR MORE INFORMATION

Corbishley, Mike. *What Do We Know about Prehistoric People?* New York: Peter Bedrick Books, 1994.

Fowler, Brenda. *Iceman: Uncovering the Life and Times of a Prehistoric Man Found in an Alpine Glacier.* New York: Random House, 2000.

Goode, Ruth. *People of the Ice Age.* New York: Crowell-Collier Press, 1973.

Hawkes, Jacquetta. *The Atlas of Early Man.* New York: St. Martin's Press, 1976.

Lambert, David, and the Diagram Group. *The Field Guide to Early Man.* New York: Facts on File, 1987.

Wilkinson, Phil, and Nick Merriman, eds. *Early Humans.* New York: Dorling Kindersley, 2000.

Prehistoric Headwear

Evidence concerning the way early man clothed and decorated his body has lasted for thousands of years, but very little has been discovered about how early humans cared for or styled their hair. Even the best-preserved bodies of ancient man reveal nothing about how hair was worn. Rock paintings from the years 15,000 to 10,000 B.C.E. found in caves in France and southern Spain show no specific hairstyles, nor do rock paintings found in the African Sahara dating from 7000 to 6000 B.C.E. Most archeologists believe that hair types were as variable as are found in humans today, with many different colors and textures of hair. It seems likely that both men and women wore their hair longer, because they lacked good tools for cutting hair. Caps of fur were probably worn to keep the head warm. Also, some of the jewelry that has been discovered seems to have been intended for holding back long hair. Men likely wore facial hair, again because of the lack of tools to remove it. If hair was cut, it was probably done with the same stone cutting tools used to chop wood and scrape animal furs.

FOR MORE INFORMATION

Lambert, David, and the Diagram Group. *The Field Guide to Early Man.* New York: Facts on File, 1987.

9

Prehistoric Body Decorations

The existence of identifiable body decorations on some Neanderthal humans from as early as 75,000 B.C.E. provides intriguing evidence of the first human use of adornment or decoration, and thus the first incidence of fashion. In the Shanidar Cave in northern Iraq, remains of Neanderthal man, an early subspecies of *Homo sapiens,* were found alongside lumps of red iron oxide and rubbed manganese. Archeologists, scientists who study the physical remains of past cultures, believe that these items were used to draw designs on the body. The red material is thought to symbolize blood, but it is not known whether the decorations were meant to attract or frighten. Cro-Magnon (another prehistoric ancestor of modern humans) burial sites dating back as far as 33,000 B.C.E. in the southwest of modern-day France also showed evidence of the use of red dyes on the body.

Some of the best direct evidence of early human body decoration comes from the rock paintings of the Sahara desert of northern Africa. The oldest of these paintings dates to about 7000 B.C.E., with other paintings dating to as late as 1500 B.C.E. The earliest and most famous of these paintings, found in the country of Algeria in northern Africa, shows a woman with parallel rows of dots running down her legs, arms, and torso. Another example of early body painting comes from headless stone female figurines found by archeologists near Ain Ghazal, Jordan. The figurines, which are believed to date back to 8000 B.C.E., featured indented patterns around the buttocks and belly. Later examples of body decoration among early humans include figurines from c. 5000 B.C.E. Mesopotamia (the region centered in present-day Iraq near the Tigris and Euphrates rivers) and 3000 B.C.E. Romania that show evidence of similar markings on the legs, arms, and breasts. Scientists believe that these markings signal a woman's fertility or ability to bear children and made

Cavemen wore fur to keep their bodies warm and protect their feet against rough terrain.
Reproduced by permission of © James W. Porter/CORBIS.

women more appealing to potential mates. The use of decoration to draw attention to a woman's sexual qualities would become one of the primary functions of fashion throughout human history.

Evidence of male body decoration is more elusive, but it seems very likely that early man also decorated his body. Given the examples of primitive peoples who survived into the modern era, including the Aborigines in Australia and Native Americans in North America, who use elaborate patterns of decoration for many occasions, scientists believe that it is likely that early man did so as well. The body was likely painted in order to provide camouflage while hunting or for ritual or social occasions. They may also have used other forms of decoration such as tattooing or scarification, in which small cuts are made in the skin to create permanent scars in patterns.

In addition to body painting and decoration, it is also clear that beginning with Neanderthal man, early humans did enjoy wearing decorative objects. The gravesites of Neanderthals indicate that both men and women liked to ornament themselves with bracelets and necklaces that consisted of a length of animal hide strung with beads, shells, teeth, bones, or other small objects.

FOR MORE INFORMATION

Gröning, Karl. *Body Decoration: A World Survey of Body Art.* New York: Vendome Press, 1998.

Lambert, David, and the Diagram Group. *The Field Guide to Early Man.* New York: Facts on File, 1987.

Powell, Jillian. *Traditions around the World: Body Decoration.* New York: Thomson Learning, 1995.

[*See also* **Volume 2, Early Asian Cultures: Tattooing; Volume 2, Oceania: Tattooing; Volume 2, Native American Cultures: Tattooing; Volume 2, African Cultures: Scarification; Volume 2, African Cultures: Siyala**]

Prehistoric Footwear

As with many other elements from the life of prehistoric humans, little can be known about the nature of footwear at that time. Archeologists, scientists who study the physical remains of past cultures, have discovered fragments of leather shoes and foot-wrappings from a variety of different locations that give some insight into how prehistoric peoples protected their feet. The oldest known shoes are ten-thousand-year-old sandals found in a desert area of eastern Oregon; other finds include eight-thousand-year-old shoes discovered in a cave in Missouri, and fragments of shoes found in Denmark that are nearly four thousand years old. However, the existence of twenty-five-thousand-year-old clothing suggests that footwear may be older than is even presently known.

The types of shoes worn by prehistoric humans depended upon the materials available to them. In northern Europe the Ice Age, which occurred approximately 1.6 million years ago, left most of the landscape frozen, leaving people little access to natural plant fibers. Shoes were typically made from the hides of deer or sheep. It appears likely that people made their shoes shortly after killing the animal, when the hide was still soft and supple, making it easier to fit to their feet. People placed their foot on the hide and cut out a shape around their foot, then wrapped the hide up to their ankle and secured it in place with strips of hide, or thongs. In North America the presence of natural plant fibers allowed people to weave more elaborate and better fitting shoes that became the predecessor to modern sandals. Anasazi, or prehistoric American Indian, shoes from the desert southwest of present-day Arizona were woven from the fibers of the yucca plant, which were very durable.

The eight-thousand-year-old shoes discovered in Missouri were made of a plant called rattlesnake master, similar to yucca. These shoes were woven in several different styles and had to stand up to hard use, claimed University of Missouri scientist Michael O'Brien in a CNN online story. O'Brien claimed, "The earliest shoe is every bit as well-made and as complex as those from later on. . . . Some of these shoes you would swear were made in a [modern] Mexican market."

Whether made from leather or from plant fibers, prehistoric shoes had to stand up to heavy usage. Lacking domesticated animals like horses, prehistoric man had to hunt, travel, and do everything on foot. Though the available evidence shows no use of color or decoration on early footwear, the elaborate weaving on some shoes seems to indicate that people did care about the appearance of the shoes.

FOR MORE INFORMATION

"8,000-Year-Old Shoes Prove Cave-Dwellers Were Well-Heeled." *CNN.com.* http://www.cnn.com/TECH/science/9807/02/prehistoric.shoes (accessed on July 24, 2003).

Hald, Margrethe. *Primitive Shoes: An Archaeological-Ethnological Study Based upon Shoe Finds from the Jutland Peninsula.* Copenhagen: National Museum of Denmark, 1972.

Ancient Egypt

Ancient Egypt is one of the most studied and best known of the early civilizations. With its great pyramids and temples that have survived to the present day, and with the fascinating mummies found in tombs filled with riches and lined with hieroglyphs, or picture drawings, ancient Egypt provides a fascinating historical record. Tracing its roots to about 4000 B.C.E., the civilizations that we know as ancient Egypt existed for nearly four thousand years before they broke up and came under the control of the Roman Empire. During its peak, from about 2700 B.C.E. to about 750 B.C.E., ancient Egypt developed a complex and powerful civilization and also created fascinating customs surrounding dress and body ornamentation.

The power of the pharaohs

The first Egyptian cultures formed along the banks of the Nile River in northern Africa sometime before 4000 B.C.E. Ever since that time, the Nile has been at the center of Egyptian culture. One of earth's great rivers, the Nile's waters allowed for the development of agriculture in a dry land, and communities formed along its banks. The Nile flows north from Lake Victoria in present-day Uganda through Sudan and into Egypt and empties into the Mediterranean Sea. In ancient times Egypt had been divided into Upper Egypt to the south and Lower Egypt to the north. In about 3100 B.C.E. the

The Pyramids at Giza in Egypt are one of the Seven Wonders of the World. *Photograph by Dilip Mehia. Reproduced by permission of Stock Market.*

two cultures were united under King Menes. (Some believe, however, the king who united the two Egypts was named King Narmer.) He became the first pharaoh, the Egyptian name for the ultimate ruler, and he wore the pschent, a crown that symbolized the union of the two regions of Egypt.

From the time of Menes on, Egypt was ruled by pharaohs whose reign was known as a dynasty. The pharaohs were thought to be directly related to the gods. In fact, Egyptians believed that the pharaohs were gods. The pharaohs had ultimate power in Egypt and were the head of the religion and the government; any decision that they made was accepted without question. The society that they ruled over fully accepted the power of the pharaoh, and Egypt was long protected from foreign attack by the vast deserts that lay to the west and the Red Sea that lay to the east. For these reasons Egyptian society was very stable. Pharaoh succeeded pharaoh for nearly three thousand years, and many elements of Egyptian culture stayed the same throughout this time, including many of their clothing traditions.

Egyptian timeline

The history of ancient Egypt is broken into several periods or eras. There are stretches of time in Egyptian society that we know more about than others. During the well-known periods, Egyptians left enduring records of their society in the form of buildings and hieroglyphs that describe the period. These times were the most stable, with peaceful succession of rulers. From the lesser-known periods, few records remain. Out of the well-known periods there are three that are extensively studied: the Old Kingdom, the Middle Kingdom, and the New Kingdom. The Old Kingdom period, which lasted from about 2700 B.C.E. to about 2000 B.C.E., saw the construction of the first great monuments of Egyptian architecture: the great stone pyramids at Giza on the west bank of the Nile near the current Egyptian capital of Cairo. During the Old Kingdom Egyptians developed an accurate solar calendar much like the one we use today, and they made great achievements in art and culture. The Middle Kingdom period lasted from about 2000 B.C.E. to about 1500 B.C.E. It is known for achievements made in literature and for the increasing contacts that Egyptians made with surrounding cultures in the greater Middle East. Egyptians borrowed customs from other cultures and incorporated them into their lives.

The New Kingdom period lasted from about 1500 B.C.E. to about 750 B.C.E. During this time Egypt truly became an empire. It conquered its neighbors to the south and expanded its control into other parts of Africa. Egypt became very rich during the New Kingdom, and it displayed its wealth in lavish temples and more highly decorated clothes. Egyptian society began to break down after about 1000 B.C.E., and it was conquered by Macedonian leader Alexander the Great (356–323 B.C.E.) in 332 B.C.E. From that point on the stable and distinctive culture of ancient Egypt slowly disappeared.

Distinctive Egyptian culture

Though ancient Egyptian culture existed for nearly thirty centuries, many elements of the culture stayed quite similar over this vast span of time. Religion remained very important to the Egyptians. Religious rituals accompanied every part of Egyptian daily life. One key belief held by Egyptians was that of eternal life. They believed that life would go on after death, so they preserved

UNRAVELING THE MYSTERY OF HIEROGLYPHS

Ever since the final decline of the ancient Egyptian Empire people have struggled to understand the detailed pictures the Egyptians used to describe their lives for more than thirty centuries. The pictures, called hieroglyphs, were everywhere in Egypt: in common tombs, on monuments and temples, and especially in the ornate burial rooms of Egyptian rulers, called pharaohs, which were contained within the great pyramids. The hieroglyphs were small pictures of common objects including feathers, lions, birds, pots, and many other items. In the time when Greeks had traded with and ruled Egypt between about 332 B.C.E. and 146 B.C.E., outsiders had known how to read the hieroglyphs, which made up a complex language. But as the Roman Empire came to power in Egypt after 146 B.C.E., the ability to understand the hieroglyphs disappeared. The hieroglyphs, and the story they told, became a great mystery that puzzled historians for nearly two thousand years.

Over the years scholars and historians tried to understand what the hieroglyphs meant. Different people offered different explanations, but no one could ever agree. Then in 1799 French soldiers stationed near the city of Rosetta, Egypt, made a great discovery. French lieutenant Pierre François Xavier Bouchard found a large gray stone that contained three different kinds of writing: Egyptian hieroglyphs, demotic script (the everyday writing of the ancient Egyptians), and Greek. Bouchard believed that the stone might hold the key to uncovering the mystery of the hieroglyphs and soon, others agreed. The stone, which became known as the Rosetta Stone, had the informa-tion needed to translate both of the lost Egyptian languages. Modern readers understood Greek and needed to make the connections between Greek, the demotic script, and the hieroglyphs, and the mystery would be solved. But it was not so easy.

In 1801 the English, who were at war with France, captured the Rosetta Stone and brought it to the British Museum in England. Egyptologists, people who study the culture of ancient Egypt, traveled to the British Museum to try to crack the code of the Rosetta Stone, pieces of which had cracked off and been lost. A well-known and gifted English doctor named Thomas Young (1773–1829) was the first to try. He translated the Greek and then tried to match patterns in that language to patterns in the two lost Egyptian languages. He discovered a great deal about how the languages worked. For example, he learned that the symbols stood for sounds and that the demotic script was closely related to the hieroglyphs. But he couldn't quite make the languages match up.

Beginning in 1807 a Frenchman named Jean François Champollion began to study the Rosetta Stone. For fifteen years he tried to break the code, racing against Young to see who would succeed first. Finally in 1822 Champollion made a breakthrough. He understood that the pictures didn't stand for the single sounds of individual letters but for more complex sounds. For example, he discovered that the hieroglyph of a bird known as an ibis stood for the Egyptian god Thoth. He substituted the sound "thoth" for the bird picture and did the same with other sounds. His plan worked. He had cracked the code of the Rosetta Stone, and people could finally understand Egyptian hieroglyphs.

dead bodies very well. Those people who could afford it had their bodies made into mummies, or bodies that were preserved and wrapped in cloth. Nobles, or high officials, and pharaohs were always well preserved and their bodies were kept in tombs that were filled with goods that they might need in the afterlife. The great

Ancient Egyptian hieroglyphics can be found inside tombs and palaces, and carved into the outside walls of buildings, such as this temple. *Reproduced by permission of © Roger Wood/CORBIS.*

Champollion traveled to Egypt to confirm his discovery. He visited vast temples whose walls were covered with hieroglyphs, and he poured over ancient scrolls of papyrus, a form of ancient paper. He was the first man to "read" the history of ancient Egypt in well over a thousand years.

Champollion made a translation dictionary and explained the grammar of Egyptian writing. Soon others learned to read the lost languages. Today we know a great deal about ancient Egypt thanks to the work of the scholars who discovered the secrets of the hieroglyphs.

pyramids and temples were the greatest of these tombs but were frequently ransacked by robbers over the ages, destroying many preserved treasures. The only pharaoh's tomb to be found intact belonged to King Tutankhamun, the young king who ruled in the fourteenth century B.C.E. His solid gold coffin and the many riches found nearby, which were discovered in 1922, show how rich the lives of these pharaohs must have been. The great pyramids of ancient Egypt, which survive to this day as a marvel of human engineering, show how seriously Egyptians took preparations for the afterlife.

The other great source of stability in ancient Egypt was the Nile River. While religion and the pharaohs controlled one aspect of life in Egypt, the Nile—the longest river in the world—controlled other aspects. Its seasonal floods richened the soil that provided the basis for Egypt's agricultural economy. Egyptians grew a variety of grains, such as wheat and flax. They also grew vegetables. All of the major settlements in Egypt were built along the Nile, for much of the rest of the area was desert. Egyptians lived in small towns, and they built homes from mud bricks which helped keep the walls cool in the hot temperatures.

In the contemporary world fashions change all the time. But in ancient Egypt certain kinds of clothing were worn by generation after generation of people with very little change. For Egyptians, this stability was not a problem but rather a symbol of the secure nature of their society.

FOR MORE INFORMATION

Batterberry, Michael, and Ariane Batterberry. *Fashion: The Mirror of History.* New York: Greenwich House, 1977.

Chrisp, Peter. *Ancient Egypt Revealed.* New York: DK Publishing, 2002.

Contini, Mila. *Fashion: From Ancient Egypt to the Present Day.* Edited by James Laver. New York: Odyssey Press, 1965.

Cosgrave, Bronwyn. *The Complete History of Costume and Fashion: From Ancient Egypt to the Present Day.* New York: Checkmark Books, 2000.

Donoughue, Carol. *The Mystery of the Hieroglyphs: The Story of the Rosetta Stone and the Race to Decipher Egyptian Hieroglyphs.* New York: Oxford University Press, 1999.

Kinnaer, Jacques. *The Ancient Egypt Site.* http://www.ancient-egypt.org (accessed on July 24, 2003).

Payne, Blanche, Geitel Winakor, and Jane Farrell-Beck. *The History of Costume.* 2nd ed. New York: HarperCollins, 1992.

Shuter, Jane. *The Ancient Egyptians.* Austin, TX: Raintree Steck-Vaughn, 2000.

Egyptian Clothing

The ancient Egyptians were the first human society to have an identifiable sense of style in clothing. From Egypt's earliest beginnings around 3100 B.C.E. to its eventual decline around 332 B.C.E., Egypt's kings and queens, called pharaohs, and its many noble men and women placed great emphasis on the appearances of their clothes, jewelry, the wigs they wore in place of natural hair, and their skin. The Egyptians idolized the human body, and the clothes they wore complimented the lines of the slender bodies that were most appreciated in Egyptian society.

Dressing for a warm climate

Egypt's climate was very warm, as it is today, and Egyptian dress provided the perfect complement to this warm weather. Both men and women tended to dress very lightly. For nearly 1,500 years it was very rare for men to wear anything on their torso, or upper body. For the upper class and the pharaohs, the main form of dress was the schenti, a simple kilt that tied around the waist and hung about to the knees. Working men wore first a loincloth, a very small garment that covered just the private parts, and later the loin skirt, which was somewhat more modest and covered from the waist to the mid thigh. In about 1500 B.C.E. Egyptian men began to wear simple tunics on their upper bodies. They adopted the custom from the neighboring region of Syria, which Egypt had recently conquered.

Women also dressed lightly, and they too often bared much of their upper body. The basic form of female clothing was a simple dress called a kalasiris. It was a tube of cloth, sewn along one side, with one or two shoulder straps. In many cases the straps extended to mid torso, leaving the breasts exposed. Less common were

The tomb of King Tutankhamen. Drawings in tombs like these helped archeologists learn what type of clothing Egyptians wore and what their daily life was like.
Reproduced by permission of Getty Images.

several other items of female clothing. Some women wore wide skirts that they combined with a close-fitting wrap with long sleeves. During the reign of King Akhenaten, from about 1379 to about 1362 B.C.E., women like the king's wife, Nefertiti, adopted long, flowing, pleated linen dresses.

The importance of linen

The single most important fabric in Egypt was linen. Linen was made from the fibers of a plant called flax. Egypt had well-developed weaving techniques, and many Egyptian workers were involved in producing linen fabrics. It was a light fabric, which made it comfortable in hot weather. It was also easy to starch, or stiffen, into pleats and folds, which decorated the clothing of both men and women, especially beginning in the Middle Kingdom (c. 2000–c. 1500 B.C.E.).

Egyptians used a variety of colors in their clothing, and these colors had symbolic meanings. Blue, for example, stood for Amon, god of air; green represented life and youth; and yellow was the symbol of gold. Red, which symbolized violence, was seldom used, and black was reserved for the wigs worn by both men and women. By far the most revered color was white. White was a sacred color among the Egyptians, symbolizing purity. Luckily, white was the natural color of flax.

Another quality of linen that was particularly appealing was its thinness. Linen could be made so thin, or sheer, that it was transparent. Egyptians were not modest and enjoyed showing off their bodies. Women and men are frequently depicted in hieroglyphs, or picture stories, wearing see-through garments.

Ideal or reality?

Our knowledge of Egyptian clothing has come almost entirely from studying the many hieroglyphs left in the tombs of kings and nobles. This has led some historians to question whether our knowledge of Egyptian clothing is based on reality or on idealized images. It seems likely that hieroglyphs would offer the best possible picture of clothing, making the colors brighter and the fit more pleasing—like photos in a fashion magazine do today. The few physical remnants of clothes that have been found are in fact heavier and more clumsy in their construction than those depicted in the hieroglyphs.

One of the facts about Egyptian clothing that has most intrigued historians is the lack of change seen in the clothing over many centuries. Basic garments such as the schenti and the kalasiris were virtually unchanged for more than twenty centuries. This lack of change has led historians Michael and Ariane Batterberry to conclude, in their book *Fashion: The Mirror of History*, that the Egyptians' costume habits shouldn't be considered fashion, which refers to styles of clothing that frequently change, but rather a symbol of this culture's consistently simple, beautiful, and enduring sense of style.

FOR MORE INFORMATION

Batterberry, Michael, and Ariane Batterberry. *Fashion: The Mirror of History*. New York: Greenwich House, 1977.

Contini, Mila. *Fashion: From Ancient Egypt to the Present Day*. Edited by James Laver. New York: Odyssey Press, 1965.

Cosgrave, Bronwyn. *The Complete History of Costume and Fashion: From Ancient Egypt to the Present Day.* New York: Checkmark Books, 2000.

Watson, Philip J. *Costume of Ancient Egypt.* New York: Chelsea House, 1987.

Kalasiris

The single most distinctive and important garment worn by women throughout the history of ancient Egypt was the kalasiris, a long linen dress. From the earliest depictions of women at the beginning of the Old Kingdom in around 2700 B.C.E. to those at the end of the New Kingdom in around 750 B.C.E., the kalasiris was the uniform of the Egyptian woman. In its earliest form, the kalasiris was a very close-fitting tube dress, sewn at the side, that was held up by two straps that attached behind the neck. The straps came together at the front and the breasts were exposed. Other versions of the dress had a single strap that went over one shoulder but were still nearly formfitting.

Costume historians caution that the depictions of the kalasiris may be idealized images, not accurate pictures of real dresses. Historians doubt whether Egyptian dressmakers would have been able to sew garments that fit bodies so perfectly. To tailor such close-fitting garments would have required great skill, and little evidence exists to prove that Egyptians possessed the knowledge needed to create such garments.

Egyptian women's garments underwent fewer changes over time than the clothes men wore. The major change with the kalasiris was that the top of the dress was extended further up the women's torso to cover her breasts. The typical kalasiris was white; however, depictions found in hieroglyphs, pictures of Egyptian life that have been preserved in tombs and on other relics that have survived to modern day, reveal that women often dyed their kalasirises in bright colors and, especially during the New Kingdom (c. 1500–c. 750), covered them with detailed patterns. Wealthy women wore kalasirises of finely woven fabric, some so thin that the dresses became transparent. When the weather grew cool they might throw a shawl over the top of their dress. Poorer women likely wore a kalasiris made from heavier, coarser fabric, and its cut was likely not as close. Kalasirises typically extended down the leg to between mid-calf and ankle length.

Interestingly, no actual examples of the kalasiris have ever been found. The depictions of the dress, however, indicate that they were made from linen, a fine-textured fabric made from the fibers of the flax plant. The ancient Egyptians used almost no other fabric to make their garments for thousands of years. Linen had many advantages for ancient Egyptians, who lived in a hot, sunny climate. It could be woven very finely, creating a light, cool fabric. Linen was also easy to wash, and in ancient Egyptian culture cleanliness was considered more important to the appearance than decoration.

FOR MORE INFORMATION

Balkwill, Richard. *Clothes and Crafts in Ancient Egypt.* Parsippany, NJ: Dillon Press, 1998.

Batterberry, Michael, and Ariane Batterberry. *Fashion: The Mirror of History.* New York: Greenwich House, 1982.

Loincloth and Loin Skirt

The most basic garment of clothing for Egyptian working men was the loincloth or loin skirt. The climate in Egypt was very hot. Many workers simply worked naked. But the hieroglyphics, or picture drawings, found in Egyptian tombs indicate that many men working in agriculture, wood, metal, leather, and tailoring wore a loincloth or a loin skirt. The loincloth was a very simple garment and is seen beginning in the Old Kingdom period (c. 2700–c. 2000 B.C.E.). Most often it consisted of a linen belt wrapped around the waist with a triangular flap of material that hung down in front of the private parts. Sometimes the hanging part of the loincloth was longer and was pulled through the legs and tucked into the back of the belt, offering more protection. Some workers wore a loincloth made of a single piece of leather. Shaped like a triangle with hide strings stretching from either end of one edge, the piece was tied around the waist and the point of the triangle was pulled up between the legs and tied at the back.

This wall painting from ancient Egypt shows how men wore loincloths in every aspect of life.
Reproduced by permission of © Historical Picture Archive/ CORBIS.

Unlike many Egyptian clothing styles, which stayed basically the same for three thousand years, the loincloth developed over time into the loin skirt. Hieroglyphs from the Middle Kingdom period of Egyptian history (c. 2000–c. 1500 B.C.E.) show male workers wearing a short skirt tied around the waist with a belt. The garment was similar to the schenti, or kilt, worn by the higher officials, called nobles. Although there is no direct evidence, the drawings from the period seem to indicate that these loin skirts may have been woven from grass or straw. These loin skirts were usually fairly short, reaching only to mid thigh, and were sometimes worn over a loincloth, the flap of which can be seen hanging down below the hem of the skirt. The loin skirt remained the clothing of choice for working men through the years of the New Kingdom (c. 1500–c. 750 B.C.E.).

FOR MORE INFORMATION

Cosgrave, Bronwyn. *The Complete History of Costume and Fashion: From Ancient Egypt to the Present Day.* New York: Checkmark Books, 2000.

Watson, Philip J. *Costume of Ancient Egypt.* New York: Chelsea House, 1987.

[*See also* **Volume 1, Ancient Egypt: Schenti**]

Penis Sheath

The penis sheath was an essential element of men's costume in ancient Egypt. This strategically placed strip of cloth was worn, not out of modesty as we might assume, but to protect what was considered a vital and sacred organ from environmental elements, working hazards, as well as troublesome insects and tropical diseases.

In ancient Egypt all men adopted costume that emphasized the front of the body. The traditional male garment, called the schenti, was a simple kilt made out of leather, hide, or linen that was wrapped around the hips. This emphasis on the genital area was due to the fact that it was regarded as sacred because of its central role in procreation. Attention was also directed to this part of the body by draping cloth from the waist over the pubic area.

Some ancient Egyptian drawings depict men naked except for a belt around the waist from which hangs a strip of cloth forming a penis sheath. Even in historical times unmarried men still walked around in this garb. During the New Kingdom (c. 1500–c. 750 B.C.E.), Egyptian military recruits donned a uniform consisting of a short kilt or merely a penis sheath, with a feather in the hair for ornament.

The penis sheath may also have inspired one of ancient Egypt's most enduring icons. The *ankh* hieroglyph means "life" and has been called the original cross. However, its origin remains a mystery. Some scholars have speculated that it represents a sacred or magical knot or a sandal strap. Still others believe the ankh sign may have a connection to the ceremonial penis sheath worn by the Egyptian king during the *heb sed,* a ritual performed every thirty years after his coronation where the king performed a ritual run and dance aimed at proving he was still physically able to rule.

FOR MORE INFORMATION

Contini, Mila. *Fashion: From Ancient Egypt to the Present Day.* Edited by James Laver. New York: Odyssey Press, 1965.

Houston, Mary G. *Ancient Egyptian, Mesopotamian, and Persian Costume.* London, England: A. C. Black, 1954.

Schenti

The schenti, or kilt, was the basic garment of the Egyptian nobleman, or upper class, from the earliest days of the Old Kingdom (c. 2700–c. 2000 B.C.E.) all the way through the New Kingdom (c. 1500–c. 750 B.C.E.). At its most basic, the schenti was a rectangular piece of cloth, wrapped around the hips and held in place by tucking one end into the tightly wrapped waist or by wearing a tied belt. Evidence of the schenti comes from the many hieroglyphs, or picture drawings, that appear in the well-preserved tombs of Egyptian nobles.

It is believed that the first schenti were made of leather or animal hides, but soon linen became the preferred fabric. Linen was made from a flax plant and was produced by a well-developed weaving industry. It was a light fabric, comfortable in the hot weather of Egypt, and it was easy to starch, or stiffen, into the pleats or folds that were favored during the Middle Kingdom (c. 2000–c. 1500 B.C.E.) and the New Kingdom.

The basic form of the schenti remained remarkably the same throughout the over two-thousand-year history of ancient Egypt. There were, however, many variations in this basic form. The first innovation in the schenti was a curved cut made at one end of the rectangular fabric, which then appeared in the front of the garment when that end was tucked into the belt. These front decorations grew more elaborate, with fringe appearing in one Old Kingdom example and vertical pleats adorning other examples. By the time of the Middle Kingdom, schenti had grown slightly longer, reaching to just below the knee. Another addition was a triangular apron that hung down the front of the schenti. The apron looked like a pyramid, with the pointy tip at the waistline and the flat base at the knee. This apron was often starched, sometimes in such a way that it projected out in front of the wearer. During the Middle Kingdom and the New Kingdom, many hieroglyphs show men wearing a longer, transparent skirt over the top of their schenti. Sometimes these skirts hung all the way to the ankles and, in some cases, were starched and pleated.

FOR MORE INFORMATION

Cosgrave, Bronwyn. *The Complete History of Costume and Fashion: From Ancient Egypt to the Present Day.* New York: Checkmark Books, 2000.

Watson, Philip J. *Costume of Ancient Egypt.* New York: Chelsea House, 1987.

Tunic

Ancient Egyptian clothing remained relatively unchanged for over two thousand years, with one important exception: the introduction of the tunic, a simple garment that covered the upper body. Egypt's hot climate meant that wearing clothing on the torso was not necessary, and throughout the Old Kingdom (c. 2700–c. 2000 B.C.E.) and the Middle Kingdom (c. 2000–c. 1500 B.C.E.) men dressed primarily in the schenti, or kilt, and sometimes with a skirt worn over the schenti. At the beginning of the New Kingdom (c. 1500–c. 750 B.C.E.), however, Egypt conquered Syria. Syrians were known for the quality of their weaving, and they helped introduce better cloth production, and the tunic, to Egypt.

At its most basic, the tunic was a long rectangular piece of fabric with a hole in the center for the head. Its open sides could be secured with a belt, and it usually extended just past the waistline. The tunic was usually worn with a schenti. Under the Egyptians,

An Egyptian man wearing a tunic. *Reproduced by permission of © Gianni Dagli Orti/CORBIS.*

however, tunic design became more detailed. The sides were sewn together, forming short sleeves that were often starched so that they stuck outward, making the shoulders appear broad. Like other linen garments, the tunic was decorated with pleats and folds and was usually bleached white.

One of the most unusual styles of clothing ever worn by Egyptians, according to fashion historian Bronwyn Cosgrave in *The Complete History of Costume and Fashion: From Ancient Egypt to the Present Day,* was an extended tunic that became a kind of robe. The rectangular fabric was more than twice as long as the wearer's height, the sleeves were very wide, and the accompanying long skirt was gathered at the waist.

FOR MORE INFORMATION

Cosgrave, Bronwyn. *The Complete History of Costume and Fashion: From Ancient Egypt to the Present Day.* New York: Checkmark Books, 2000.

Payne, Blanche, Geitel Winakor, and Jane Farrell-Beck. *The History of Costume.* 2nd ed. New York: HarperCollins, 1992.

Watson, Philip J. *Costume of Ancient Egypt.* New York: Chelsea House, 1987.

Egyptian Headwear

The ancient Egyptians cared very much about their appearance. They wore finely tailored and flattering clothes and took great care of their bodies. It is often considered strange then that the wealthiest Egyptians–both men and women–shaved themselves bald. Evidence indicates that being clean shaven on the head and face was a sign of nobility, and copper razors found in the tombs of upperclass Egyptians reveal the importance of staying clean shaven. Archeologists, scientists who study the distant past using physical evidence, also believe that Egyptians shaved to keep themselves cool in the hot Egyptian climate.

Though some Egyptians shaved themselves bald, they still cared about having a pleasing hairstyle, and so they wore a variety of stylish wigs. Egyptians were skilled wig makers. They made wigs out of human hair and bound the wigs to their heads with various headbands and headdresses. By the time of the New Kingdom (c. 1500–c. 750 B.C.E.), wigs had become very ornamental and were woven with gold and jewels. Poorer Egyptians, however, wore wigs made from wool. Male Egyptian rulers sometimes wore beard wigs during special ceremonies.

Not all Egyptians shaved and wore wigs, however. Hairstyles were used to show a person's position in society. Young children had their hair cut short, except for a long strand called a side-lock that hung from the right side of the head. Married women also had a distinctive hairstyle. They wore their hair with bangs (hair covering the forehead) and shoulder length locks at the sides and longer locks in the back. This is called the triparti style because of the three different lengths of hair. Hairstyles did change considerably over the long history of ancient Egypt. The hieroglyphs, drawings that tell stories of the Egyptian past, indicate that long and short hair was popular for both men and women at different times. One style that was popular throughout Egyptian history for both sexes was to have long hair that was combed behind the ears and then in front of the shoulders, creating an attractive frame for the face.

In addition to wigs and varying hairstyles, Egyptians wore different types of hats and headdresses. At the peak of Egyptian society, the ruler, called a pharaoh, wore the distinctive double crown known as a pschent. Other forms of headwear were worn for specific ceremonies. Many of the ceremonial hats were decorated with a figure of the uraeus, a sacred hooded cobra. Especially during the New Kingdom period, Egyptians used jewels and elaborate braiding, similar to cornrows, to decorate their heads.

FOR MORE INFORMATION

Batterberry, Michael, and Ariane Batterberry. *Fashion: The Mirror of History.* New York: Greenwich House, 1977.

Contini, Mila. *Fashion: From Ancient Egypt to the Present Day.* Edited by James Laver. New York: Odyssey Press, 1965.

Corson, Richard. *Fashions in Hair: The First Five Thousand Years.* London, England: Peter Owen, 2001.

Cosgrave, Bronwyn. *The Complete History of Costume and Fashion: From Ancient Egypt to the Present Day.* New York: Checkmark Books, 2000.

Trasko, Mary. *Daring Do's: A History of Extraordinary Hair.* New York: Flammarion, 1994.

Watson, Philip J. *Costume of Ancient Egypt.* New York: Chelsea House, 1987.

Headdresses

Egyptian aristocrats and pharaohs, or emperors, wore a wide variety of headdresses. Egyptians often wore wigs to protect themselves from the heat of the climate, and they likely wore headdresses for the same reason. Many of the headdresses depicted in the hieroglyphics, or picture drawings, found in Egyptian tombs indicate that headdresses also had a ceremonial purpose. The pschent, worn by the pharaoh to symbolize his or her power over all of Egypt, was the most famous headdress, but there were many others.

One of the most common forms of headdress was the nemes headcloth. This stiff linen headdress covered the head and most often had flaps that hung down the sides and over the shoulders. The nemes headcloth was often full of bright colors. It put a frame around the face and is famous as the type of headdress worn by King Tutankhamen, who ruled Egypt in the fourteenth century B.C.E. and whose gold casket was discovered in 1922 and has been displayed around the world. Another common headdress was the simple headband. Made of linen or perhaps even of leather inlaid with gold, the main purpose of this headdress was to hold the wearer's wig in place.

Pharaohs are also depicted wearing a headdress known as the Blue Crown, or khepresh. This tall crown was likely made of stiff linen or leather and spread up and back from the forehead six to eight inches. It was blue, covered in small circular studs, and often had a carved uraeus, a sacred hooded cobra ornament, on the front and two long streamers hanging down the back. A famous crown was also worn by Queen Nefertiti, who ruled briefly around 1330 B.C.E. This blue, cone-shaped hat tapered down and covered her skull. It was banded with a decorative stripe and had a menacing uraeus at its front.

Burial mask of King Tutankhamen showing the king wearing a nemes headdress. *Reproduced by permission of Getty Images.*

Many other forms of headdress have been found, most of which were associated with the various pharaohs who ruled Egypt over its long history. These headdresses often had ornaments with symbolic meanings, such as ostrich feathers to honor Osiris, the god of the underworld, or ram horns to honor Khnum, the god who created life.

FOR MORE INFORMATION

Balkwill, Richard. *Clothes and Crafts in Ancient Egypt.* Milwaukee, WI: Gareth Stevens, 2000.

Cosgrave, Bronwyn. *The Complete History of Costume and Fashion: From Ancient Egypt to the Present Day.* New York: Checkmark Books, 2000.

"Royal Crowns." *Egyptology Online.* http://www.egyptologyonline.com/
pharaoh's_crowns.htm (accessed on July 24, 2003).

Watson, Philip J. *Costume of Ancient Egypt.* New York: Chelsea House, 1987.

[*See also* **Volume 1, Ancient Egypt: Pschent**]

Pschent

The single most important piece of headwear in all of Egyptian history was the pschent, the crown of Upper and Lower Egypt. Historians believe that Upper Egypt (surrounding the upper Nile River in the south of present-day Egypt and in Sudan) and Lower Egypt (most of present-day Egypt) were united in about 3100 B.C.E. by King Menes. The rulers of Upper and Lower Egypt each wore a different type of crown. The White Crown of Upper Egypt, known as the hedjet, was a white helmet that was shaped much like half a football with a stretched out, rounded end. It also had a coiled uraeus, or sacred hooded cobra, just above the forehead. The Red Crown of Lower Egypt, known as the deshret, was a round, flat-topped hat that extended down the back of the neck and had a tall section that projected upward from the back side. From the base of the projection a thin reed curled up and forward, ending in a spiral. When King Menes united the two Egypts, he combined the hat into the pschent, or Double Crown. The pschent had as its base the Red Crown, which completely covered the wearer's hair. The White Crown emerged out of the top of the Red Crown.

From the time of King Menes on, nearly every pharaoh from the Old Kingdom (c. 2700–c. 2000 B.C.E.), Middle Kingdom (c. 2000–c. 1500 B.C.E.), and New Kingdom (c. 1500–c. 750 B.C.E.) is depicted wearing the pschent in hieroglyphs, pictures of Egyptian life that are preserved in tombs. The pschent symbolized the power of the pharaohs who ruled over one of the greatest empires of the ancient world.

FOR MORE INFORMATION

Cosgrave, Bronwyn. *The Complete History of Costume and Fashion: From Ancient Egypt to the Present Day.* New York: Checkmark Books, 2000.

"Royal Crowns." *Egyptology Online.* http://www.egyptologyonline.com /pharaoh's_crowns.htm (accessed on July 24, 2003).

Watson, Philip J. *Costume of Ancient Egypt.* New York: Chelsea House, 1987.

[*See also* Volume 1, Ancient Egypt: Unraveling the Mystery of Hieroglyphs box on p. 18]

Wigs

Upper-class Egyptian men and women considered wigs an essential part of their wardrobe. Wearing a wig signaled a person's rank in Egyptian society. Although a shaved head was a sign of nobility during most of the Egyptian kingdoms, the majority of Egyptians kept their heads covered. Wigs were worn in place of headdresses or, for special occasions, with elaborate headdresses. Egyptian law prohibited slaves and servants from shaving their heads or wearing wigs.

The base of an Egyptian wig was a fiber-netting skullcap, with strands of human hair, wool, flax, palm fibers, felt, or other materials attached. The wig hair often stuck straight out from the skullcap, creating large, full wigs that offered wearers protection from the heat of the sun. Most often black, wigs were also other colors. Queen Nefertiti, who lived during the fourteenth century B.C.E., was known for wearing dark blue wigs, and festive wigs were sometimes gilded, or thinly coated in gold.

Wig hair was arranged in decorative styles throughout all the kingdoms of Egypt. During the earliest dynasties (which began around 3200 B.C.E.) and the Old Kingdom of Egypt (c. 2700–c. 2000 B.C.E.), both men and women wore closely cropped wigs with

This man and woman are wearing traditional Egyptian wigs. *Reproduced by permission of © Gianni Dagli Orti/CORBIS.*

rows of short curls or slightly longer straight hair. In later kingdoms, some women began to grow their hair longer and wore wigs of greater length and bulk that showed their natural hair beneath. By the time of the Middle Kingdom (c. 2000–c. 1500 B.C.E.), bulky wigs with hair coils draping forward over each shoulder were favored. During the New Kingdom (c. 1500–c. 750 B.C.E.) men's wigs became much longer in the front than in the back and less bulky, but women's wigs became larger, completely covering the shoulders. For special occasions, wigs were decorated with gold, braided with colorful ribbons, or adorned with beads. Wigs were made even more elaborate with the addition of golden bands, caps, and fancy headbands.

The hot climate of Egypt made it uncomfortable for men to wear beards. However, Egyptians believed that the beard was manly, so they developed artificial beards, or beard wigs. Men of royal rank tied stubby beards on their chins for official or festive occasions. The king's beard was longer than that of other men and was usually worn straight and thick. Gods were depicted with thinner beards that curled up at the tip. Egyptians believed that kings were descended from the gods, and in some ceremonies kings would wear a curved beard to show that they represented gods.

FOR MORE INFORMATION

Bigelow, Marybelle S. *Fashion in History: Apparel in the Western World.* Minneapolis, MN: Burgess, 1970.

Lister, Margot. *Costume: An Illustrated Survey from Ancient Time to the Twentieth Century.* London, England: Herbert Jenkins, 1967.

Payne, Blanche, Geitel Winakor, and Jane Farrell-Beck. *The History of Costume: From Ancient Mesopotamia Through the Twentieth Century.* 2nd ed. New York: HarperCollins, 1992.

Egyptian Body Decorations

Ancient Egyptians took great care with their bodies, from the way they dressed to the ornaments that they wore. The many ways that Egyptians decorated their bodies reveal their fascination with appearances. Caring for the skin was very important, especially to wealthy people. Egyptians washed their bodies often using fairly harsh soaps that stripped oils from the skin. To soften their skin they used a variety of ointments and creams. These might contain scents to perfume their bodies. The Egyptian climate was very hot, and many Egyptians shaved their heads and their facial hair. Presenting a smooth, almost polished body surface was considered a sign of high status. Historians believe that the Egyptians may have invented some of the world's first grooming products, from deodorants to toothpaste, in order to improve their smell and appearance.

Egyptians used different kinds of makeup to paint their faces and bodies. Kohl, a black pigment, was the best-known form of makeup, and it was used by people of all classes to outline the eyes. Both women and men paid special attention to their eyes and used eye makeup to protect themselves from evil and to honor the goddess Hathor, the mother of the world. Eyes were typically made up with black kohl or green malachite powder, made from a mineral found in nearby mountains. Egyptians also used red makeup for their lips and rouge, or a reddish powder, for the cheeks. Evidence of many other forms of makeup has been found in tombs and depicted in hieroglyphs, the picture language that reveals so much about Egyptian history. It appears that Egyptians may have used wrinkle treatments and painted their nails as well.

Another way that Egyptians ornamented themselves was through the use of jewelry. The best-known pieces of jewelry were the highly decorated collars and pectorals (jewelry that was hung

This sculpture of Queen Nefertiti shows her adorned in a decorative headdress and jeweled collar, representative of what Egyptian royalty wore. *Reproduced by permission of © Francis G. Mayer/CORBIS.*

over the chest by a chain around the neck) that both men and women wore on their upper chest, under and around their neck. Many other forms of jewelry were worn, including necklaces, earrings, bracelets, and rings. Wealthy women might sew jewels into the fabric of their kalasirises, or long dresses.

The ruling pharaohs, kings and queens, wore special ornaments of their own, and these ornaments were filled with symbolism. Nearly every Egyptian pharaoh carried the crook and flail, symbols of the rule of the king. The crook was similar to a tool used by shepherds, a long staff with a hook at the end. The flail was a wooden rod with three straps hanging from one end, each strap bearing decorative pendants. Another ornament carried or worn by many pharaohs was the ankh, a symbol of life that looked like a cross with a loop for its upper vertical arm, whose origins are a mystery to historians.

FOR MORE INFORMATION

Cosgrave, Bronwyn. *The Complete History of Costume and Fashion: From Ancient Egypt to the Present Day.* New York: Checkmark Books, 2000.

Watson, Philip J. *Costume of Ancient Egypt.* New York: Chelsea House, 1987.

Collars and Pectorals

While the people of ancient Egypt mostly wore plain white linen clothing of simple design, this did not mean that they had no love of adornment. Two of the most notable items of jewelry worn in ancient Egypt were collars and pectorals, both types of heavily jeweled necklaces. Collars were created with beads made of glass, precious stones, gold, and a glazed pottery called faience. These beads were strung on multiple strings of varying length that were then bound to a ring around the neck to make a wide, semicircular collar that covered the shoulders and chest of the wearer with bright color. Collars were also sometimes made by attaching beads, stones, and precious metals to a semicircle of fabric. The pectoral was usually a large, flat breastplate made of gold or copper, often decorated with symbols and inlaid with precious stones or glass. Pectorals were hung over the chest by a chain around the neck. Both collars and pectorals were worn by men and women alike.

Egyptians who could afford it wore brightly colored jewelry to show their rank and importance in society, as well as their love of beauty. Many items of jewelry served a spiritual purpose as well, by carrying images of the gods that protected the wearer. Collars often had symbols of the gods carved into their large metal clasps or into the beads of the collar itself. Pectorals were frequently adorned with symbolic pictures of gods and goddesses or were made in the shape of sacred symbols, such as winged scarab beetles or disks that represented the sun. Pectorals were considered amulets, or good luck charms, and were sometimes awarded to loyal servants of the ruling pharaoh in return for services performed. Elaborate jeweled collars and pectorals have frequently been found in the ruins of Egyptian tombs.

FOR MORE INFORMATION

Balkwill, Richard. *Clothes and Crafts in Ancient Egypt.* Milwaukee, WI: Gareth Stevens, 2000.

Black, J. Anderson, and Madge Garland. Updated and revised by Frances Kennett. *A History of Fashion.* New York: William Morrow, 1980.

Fragrant Oils and Ointments

"The Egyptians," write fashion historians Michael and Ariane Batterberry in *Fashion: The Mirror of History,* "were as clean as any people in history." They bathed regularly, shaved their bodies of any excess hair, including that on the head, and used fragrant oils and ointments to keep their skin smooth and sweet smelling. The first female queen of Egypt, Queen Netocris, who is believed to have ruled around 2170 B.C.E., recommended regular bathing and scrubbing with a paste of clay and ashes. To return natural oils to the skin, Egyptians applied one of many types of oily preparations to their bodies. These oils were made from animal fat, castor oil, or olive oil, and they were scented with flowers or other plants. Evidence indicates that many Egyptians used such oils, including workmen and soldiers. Egyptians also prepared simple perfumes made from oils and fragrant flowers and seeds.

One of the more interesting ways to apply oils and fragrance to the body came in the form of a wax or grease cone worn on the head. Hieroglyphics, or picture stories often found in Egyptian tombs, show noble women (those born to the upper classes of society) wearing cones of grease or wax on their heads. These cones would slowly melt in the Egyptian heat, bathing the wearer's head, shoulders, and arms in the perfumes held in the cone, and leaving the skin oily and glistening. Luckily, most Egyptians shaved their heads and wore wigs, so they could easily remove their hair for cleaning.

FOR MORE INFORMATION

Balkwill, Richard. *Clothes and Crafts in Ancient Egypt.* Milwaukee, WI: Gareth Stevens, 2000.

Batterberry, Michael, and Ariane Batterberry. *Fashion: The Mirror of History.* New York: Greenwich House, 1977.

Contini, Mila. *Fashion: From Ancient Egypt to the Present Day.* Edited by James Laver. New York: Odyssey Press, 1965.

Jewelry

One of the most important ways that people in ancient Egypt showed their wealth and status was through the display of jewelry. In the early stages of Egyptian civilization known as the

Old Kingdom (c. 2700–c. 2000 B.C.E.), jewelry was quite simple, consisting primarily of beaded collars worn by the very wealthy. By the time of the New Kingdom (c. 1500–c. 750 B.C.E.), however, as conquering Egyptian armies came into contact with surrounding areas of the Middle East, jewelry became more common and more complex. A variety of tombs, both from the upper classes and from kings, or pharaohs, such as King Tutankhamen, who ruled briefly in the fourteenth century B.C.E. and whose tomb was discovered in 1922, reveal that Egyptians loved all types of jewelry, but especially gold.

Egyptians adorned all parts of their body with jewels. They wore anklets, bracelets, armlets, and necklaces. These might contain strings of beads, shells, or precious and semiprecious stones, including gold, pearl, agate, and onyx. The tomb of Queen Amanishakheto, who is believed to have ruled at the very end of the Egyptian Empire, in about 10 B.C.E., revealed that the queen wore stacks of bracelets. She also had several rings, some of which she wore attached to her hair. Women also wore crowns, breastplates, and dangling earrings.

Gold was a favorite material of the Egyptians. According to Mila Contini, author of *Fashion: From Ancient Egypt to the Present Day,* gold was "thought of as the brilliant and incorruptible flesh of the Sun" and was believed to have the power to offer eternal survival. Kings and queens were buried in golden masks to guarantee their immortality. Though many of the tombs of Egyptian pharaohs were robbed over the centuries, the tomb of King Tutankhamen, or King Tut, revealed the fascination with gold. King Tut was buried in three coffins, the outer two covered in gold leaf and the inner coffin made of solid gold.

FOR MORE INFORMATION

Batterberry, Michael, and Ariane Batterberry. *Fashion: The Mirror of History.* New York: Greenwich House, 1977.

Contini, Mila. *Fashion: From Ancient Egypt to the Present Day.* Edited by James Laver. New York: Odyssey Press, 1965.

Cosgrave, Bronwyn. *The Complete History of Costume and Fashion: From Ancient Egypt to the Present Day.* New York: Checkmark Books, 2000.

[*See also* **Volume 1, Ancient Egypt: Collars and Pectorals**]

Kohl

Kohl is a black powdery substance made from galena, an ore that is the source of the mineral lead. Galena ore was found near the Nile River at the city of Aswan, in present-day southeast Egypt, and on the banks of the Red Sea, among other places. Egyptian rulers sent expeditions to bring back the ore, which was made into sticks of the dark powder and used to make thick dark lines around the eyes. Cosmetics were an important part of the ancient Egyptian costume, and rich and poor alike used kohl to darken their eyes. The kohl used by poorer workers was made in sticks, while the wealthy kept their kohl in ornate boxes made of precious materials and often carved in beautiful shapes. Small amounts of kohl were taken from the box and mixed with animal fats to make it easier to paint on the face.

This wall painting of Queen Nefertiti shows her eyes outlined in the deep black kohl worn in ancient Egypt. *Reproduced by permission of © Christel Gerstenberg/CORBIS.*

In ancient Egypt kohl was used as a cosmetic to outline the eyes with a dramatic black line. While makeup was valued as a beauty aid, most cosmetics had other uses as well. The dark eyeliner gave some protection from the bright Egyptian sun, and the galena also helped to keep insects away from the eyes. Kohl had a religious purpose, too. Ancient Egyptians used large drawings of an eye to symbolize the eye of the god Horus—the Egyptian god of healing, among other things—and believed that the drawings would protect them. Many historians think that Egyptians believed that outlining their own eyes would help them carry the protection of the gods with them. Kohl became a popular cosmetic once again during the 1920s, when an "Egyptian look" came into fashion in the United States and Europe, and it is still used as eyeliner in many Eastern countries.

FOR MORE INFORMATION

Balkwill, Richard. *Clothes and Crafts in Ancient Egypt.* Milwaukee, WI: Gareth Stevens, 2000.

Harris, Nathaniel. *Everyday Life in Ancient Egypt.* Danbury, CT: Franklin Watts, 1994.

Egyptian Footwear

For more than half of the recorded history of ancient Egypt there is almost no record of the use of footwear. The main source of evidence for this period, the pictorial stories found in tombs known as hieroglyphs, showed every class of person, from the ruling pharaoh (king or queen), to the lowly worker, going barefoot. This may not mean that people never wore some foot protection, but it does seem to indicate that footwear was of very little importance.

Historians are not sure why sandals were suddenly introduced but, beginning at the start of the New Kingdom period of Egyptian history in about 1500 B.C.E., sandals suddenly began to appear on the hieroglyphs depicting scenes of Egyptian life. Egyptians had developed advanced shoemaking skills for their time, and they created sandals woven of reeds or leather that were quite similar in design to many modern sandals.

Though the design of Egyptian sandals was simple, the wealthy still found ways to adorn them. Some had buckles on the straps made of precious metals, while others had jewels embedded in the woven soles. Some sandal designs had turned up toes, probably to keep sand out of the shoe as the wearer walked.

There is very little evidence of the use of covered shoes in ancient Egypt. The few that have been found were woven from palm fiber and grass. Such shoes seem to have been prized possessions. Sometimes travelers removed their shoes to keep them safe while they were on the road and then put them on again at journey's end. Other shoes have been found in tombs, indicating that they were important items to the dead person.

FOR MORE INFORMATION

Balkwill, Richard. *Clothes and Crafts in Ancient Egypt.* Milwaukee, WI: Gareth Stevens, 2000.

Cosgrave, Bronwyn. *The Complete History of Costume and Fashion: From Ancient Egypt to the Present Day.* New York: Checkmark Books, 2000.

Payne, Blanche, Geitel Winakor, and Jane Farrell-Beck. *The History of Costume.* 2nd ed. New York: HarperCollins, 1992.

[*See also* **Volume 1, Ancient Egypt:** Unraveling the Mystery of Hieroglyphs box on p. 18]

Sandals

One of the very earliest hieroglyphs, or picture stories of ancient Egypt found preserved in tombs, shows a sandal maker accompanying King Menes, the Egyptian ruler who united Upper and Lower Egypt in about 3100 B.C.E. Despite this evidence, most hieroglyphs show that Egyptians during the Old Kingdom period (c. 2700–c. 2000 B.C.E.) and the Middle Kingdom period (c. 2000–c. 1500 B.C.E.) went barefoot. Beginning in the New Kingdom period (c. 1500–c. 750 B.C.E.), however, sandals became the favored form of footwear. Sandals protected the feet from the hot desert sand, but their open tops allowed the feet to stay cool. They were certainly worn by nobles and pharaohs, high officials and kings and queens, though working people may still have gone barefoot.

A pair of leather Egyptian sandals. *Reproduced by permission of © Gianni Dagli Orti/CORBIS.*

The sandals worn by ancient Egyptians were very simple. They had a base that was made of wood, goatskin, or fibers from palm trees or the papyrus plant. They were held to the foot by simple straps, one of which crossed the arch of the foot and the other that went from the arch strap between the big toe and the second toe. Many of the sandals that have been discovered come to a point in front of the toes.

More elaborate sandals have been discovered in the tombs of some of the pharaohs. The tomb of King Tutankhamen, who ruled briefly in the fourteenth century B.C.E. and whose tomb was discovered in 1922, contained several pairs of sandals, including a jeweled pair and a pair with soles that were imprinted with images of his enemies. The images were meant to convey that when King Tutankhamen walked on these sandals he crushed his enemies underfoot.

FOR MORE INFORMATION

Cosgrave, Bronwyn. *The Complete History of Costume and Fashion: From Ancient Egypt to the Present Day.* New York: Checkmark Books, 2000.

Payne, Blanche, Geitel Winakor, and Jane Farrell-Beck. *The History of Costume.* 2nd ed. New York: HarperCollins, 1992.

[*See also* **Volume 1, Ancient Egypt: Unraveling the Mystery of Hieroglyphs box on p. 18**]

Mesopotamia

Between 3000 B.C.E. and 300 B.C.E. the civilizations thriving in Mesopotamia, a large region centered between the Tigris and Euphrates Rivers in modern-day Iraq, laid the foundation for customs that would dominate later European culture. Though many different societies emerged and organized cities, states, and empires in Mesopotamia, historians study these cultures together because they lived near each other and had many similarities. The main civilizations were the Sumerians (3000–2000 B.C.E.), the Akkadians (2350–2218 B.C.E.), the Babylonians (1894–1595 B.C.E.), the Assyrians (1380–612 B.C.E.), and the Persians (550–330 B.C.E.).

The people of Mesopotamia

The Sumerians created the earliest civilization in Mesopotamia around 3000 B.C.E. Large city-states developed near the Euphrates River. Some of the cities grew to have populations near 35,000 citizens. Although most Sumerians made their living by farming, professionals, such as doctors, organized into powerful associations. Both rich and poor Sumerians were considered citizens, and slaves could earn money and buy their freedom. While men enjoyed the most power in society, women in Sumeria held power in their families and a ruler's wife had authority in the government of a city-state.

A Mesopotamian alabaster figurine. *Reproduced by permission of © David Lees/CORBIS.*

Living among the Sumerians for many years, the Akkadians took power of Mesopotamia around 2350 B.C.E. Little evidence is available to describe the Akkadian culture, but it is believed to have resembled the Sumerian culture but differed in language and ethnicity. Sumerians reclaimed control of the region after about two hundred years of domination by the Akkadians and others. Under the restored Sumerian rule, Mesopotamia was again dominated by thriving agriculturally-based cities.

By 1894 B.C.E. the Babylonians rose to power in Mesopotamia. Babylonians created a thriving, organized society. Under the rule of Hammurabi (1792–1750 B.C.E.), the king of Babylon, a code of laws was developed and written down. Although evidence exists that Babylonians sold clothing and perfumes in stores, little is known about what Babylonians actually wore. While there are some depictions of the king, which indicate that he dressed in styles very similar to the Sumerians, no pictures of Babylonian women exist. The Babylonian Empire fell in about 1595 B.C.E.

Assyrians had prospered in Mesopotamia for many centuries, but by 911 B.C.E. the society began conquering surrounding areas and united Mesopotamia into one enormous empire that encompassed the Taurus Mountains of modern-day Turkey, the Mediterranean coast, and portions of Egypt. To hold their empire together, the Assyrians aggressively protected their territory and battled constantly with enemies. At the same time as they multiplied and defended their conquests, Assyrians built cities with large buildings and statues. Assyrian society was controlled by men, and women were legally inferior to them. Although the Assyrians built strong economic ties over a vast territory, they ruled brutally and the conquered nations celebrated when the Assyrians were overthrown in 612 B.C.E.

After the Assyrians were conquered, the Persian Empire rose to prominence. The Persian Empire, which united approximately twenty different societies, became known for its efficiency and its kindness to its citizens. Under Persian rule products such as clothing, money, and furniture were made in vast quantities.

How much do we really know?

The artifacts left by these cultures include clay and stone statues, carvings on palace walls, carved ivory, some wall paintings, and jewelry. These items illustrate the clothing, hairdressing, and body adornment of these cultures as well as how these cultures idealized the human form. While these visual forms provide costume historians with a great deal of information, of even greater interest are the written tablets that have been discovered. The development of written language in Mesopotamia provides historians and archeologists, scientists who study past cultures, with information about daily life in the distant past. Descriptions of how the people of Mesopotamia acted toward one another, how they dressed and cleaned themselves, how they prepared for weddings, how they organized businesses, and how they ruled by law are among the things that are recorded in written language.

But even with this information, it is impossible to know if we truly understand what the people of Mesopotamia looked like or exactly what they wore. The statues made by sculptors offer simplified depictions of people and their clothing, making it difficult to know the type of fabric used in a particular garment. In addition, different cultures portrayed people in different ways. The Sumerians created statues and pictures of stocky, large-eyed people while the Assyrians depicted people as lean, strong, and hairy. It is impossible to know if these people actually looked different from one another or if these artifacts represent the idealized version of different cultures.

FOR MORE INFORMATION

Nemet-Nejat, Karen Rhea. *Daily Life in Ancient Mesopotamia.* Westport, CT: Greenwood Press, 1998.

Payne, Blanche. *History of Costume: From the Ancient Egyptians to the Twentieth Century.* New York: Harper and Row, 1965.

Mesopotamian Clothing

The civilizations that developed in Mesopotamia near the Tigris and Euphrates Rivers between 3000 and 300 B.C.E. developed impressive skills for fashioning clothing. The evidence of these civilizations' clothing remains on sculptures, pottery, and in writings left on tablets and royal tombs. It indicates that a thriving textile or fabric industry existed in the early civilizations of Mesopotamia, which included the Sumerians (3000–2000 B.C.E.), the Akkadians (2350–2218 B.C.E.), the Babylonians (1894–1595 B.C.E.), the Assyrians (1380–612 B.C.E.), and the Persians (550–330 B.C.E.). Textiles were used for trade purposes and were also given as gifts to kings and queens.

Although the earliest civilizations used animal skins to protect themselves from the environment, people soon learned how to pound wool and goat hair into felt or weave it into cloth. Wool was the most common fabric used to make clothing in Mesopotamia and was used for practically every type of garment from cloaks to shoes. Looms for weaving fabric were in use as early as 3000 B.C.E. The skill of early weavers is extraordinary. Some fragments of linen discovered in royal tombs are almost as finely woven as modern-day linen fabric. Linen was a more luxurious fabric and was woven for the clothing of the wealthy, priests, and to adorn statues of gods. Other finely woven fabrics also became available for the wealthiest in Mesopotamia. Soft cotton was introduced in Assyria around 700 B.C.E., and silk became available later.

The surviving evidence does not show the colors of clothing made in Mesopotamia, but archeologists, scientists who study past civilizations, have discovered letters that describe how dyes, appliqués, embroidery, and beads were used to beautify garments. As early as 1200 B.C.E. a type of shell known as Maoris produced a highly-prized dye called Tyrian purple. Artifacts found in royal

A detail showing Mesopotamian clothing. *Reproduced by permission of © Gianni Dagli Orti/CORBIS.*

tombs provide evidence of fitted sewn garments, gold appliqués, and elaborately decorated clothes.

What they wore

The earliest evidence of civilization in Mesopotamia is identified as Sumerian. Early Sumerian men typically wore waist strings or small loincloths that provided barely any coverage. However, later the wraparound skirt was introduced, which hung to the knee or lower and was held up by a thick, rounded belt that tied in the back. These skirts were typically decorated with fringe or pieces of fabric cut in a petal shape. All classes of men seem to have worn these skirts. Early Sumerian women seem to have worn only a shawl wrapped around their bodies. These shawls were often decorated with simple border patterns or allover patterns. Later Sumerian women typically wore sewn outfits covered with tiers of fringe. These included skirts much like those worn by men and shawls or tops that were also fringed. By the end of Sumerian rule around 2000 B.C.E. both men and women wore skirts and shawls.

There is less evidence about what men and women wore during Babylonian rule from 1894 to 1595 B.C.E. The scant evidence available suggests that Babylonians wore skirts and shawls very similar to the Sumerians, although some men during Babylonian rule did wear loin skirts with a hemline that slanted from the upper knee in the front to the calf in the back. Evidence does suggest that the fringe on garments became more elaborate during this time. One painting discovered shows a king wearing a skirt with tiered fringe that is alternately colored red, gray, gold, and white. No evidence of female attire exists except for what was depicted in renditions of goddesses. Goddesses were shown wearing sleeved dresses with fitted bodices, V necks, and straight skirts.

The Assyrians, who ruled from 1380 to 612 B.C.E., continued to wear fringed garments. Both men and women wrapped fringed shawls over their shoulders and around their waists to cover themselves from their shoulders to nearly their ankles. These were held in place by belts. Around 1000 B.C.E. Assyrian men began wearing belted knee-length tunics with short sleeves. Men of high status, such as kings and military officers, also wore woolen cloaks dyed blue, red, purple, or white. After the Assyrians were conquered in 612 B.C.E., the Persian Empire began to prosper and people in Mesopotamia adopted Persian trousers into their wardrobes.

FOR MORE INFORMATION

Nemet-Nejat, Karen Rhea. *Daily Life in Ancient Mesopotamia.* Westport, CT: Greenwood Press, 1998.

Payne, Blanche. *History of Costume: From the Ancient Egyptians to the Twentieth Century.* New York: Harper and Row, 1965.

Fringe

Across all the civilizations living in Mesopotamia (the region centered in present-day Iraq near the Tigris and Euphrates Rivers) from 3000 to 300 B.C.E., fringe was a popular and important decorative adornment for the clothing of both men and women. It is believed that fringe was worn by all classes of people. The evidence for how fringe was used and what it looked like is found on sculptures, statues, and described in the writings left by these civilizations.

Fringe adorned the two most basic garments worn in Mesopotamia: the skirt and the shawl. These garments were made out of woven wool or linen, and later, for the wealthiest people, cotton or silk. The hems, or edges, of skirts and shawls were decorated with fringe that either hung straight or was knotted into elaborate designs. Fringe could be cut from the whole piece of cloth that made up the skirt or shawl or it could be a separate piece sewn onto the garment.

In later civilizations of Mesopotamia the fringe on garments became more and more decorative and elaborate. Fringe could be dyed many colors and layered in tiers to cover entire garments. Some men would use the fringe of their shawls as a type of signature for contracts. Instead of using a seal to impress their mark on a clay contract, men would use their unique fringe. Fringe has been used for decoration at other points in human history, notably as decoration on the leather clothes of cowboys in the American West and as a brief fashion trend in the 1970s.

FOR MORE INFORMATION

Nemet-Nejat, Karen Rhea. *Daily Life in Ancient Mesopotamia.* Westport, CT: Greenwood Press, 1998.

Payne, Blanche. *History of Costume: From the Ancient Egyptians to the Twentieth Century.* New York: Harper and Row, 1965.

[*See also* **Volume 3, Nineteenth Century: American Cowboy box on p. 614; Volume 5, 1961–79: Fringe**]

Shawl

For the men and women living in Mesopotamia (the region centered in present-day Iraq near the Tigris and Euphrates Rivers) from 3000 to 300 B.C.E., a fringed shawl was a typical garment. Unlike modern-day shawls that are worn over the shoulders and head, the shawls of Mesopotamia were wrapped around the hips like long skirts or wrapped around the torso with one end tossed over the left shoulder, covering the body to the feet like a dress. Whether worn as a skirt or a dress, shawls were held in place with belts tied in the back.

The first depictions of shawls on statues and bas-reliefs, or wall carvings, on the remains of palace walls show rather plain fabric wraps. In time, however, the fringe and decorative borders of these shawls became more elaborate. Shawls were made most commonly out of wool, but wealthy people could afford finely woven linen, and after 700 B.C.E., perhaps even cotton or silk. The wealthiest people also wore embroidered shawls or shawls decorated with gold or precious stone beads.

FOR MORE INFORMATION

Nemet-Nejat, Karen Rhea. *Daily Life in Ancient Mesopotamia.* Westport, CT: Greenwood Press, 1998.

Payne, Blanche. *History of Costume: From the Ancient Egyptians to the Twentieth Century.* New York: Harper and Row, 1965.

Mesopotamian Headwear

Men and women adorned their heads in very different ways in Mesopotamia, situated in the region centered in modern-day Iraq near the Tigris and Euphrates Rivers between 3000 and 300 B.C.E. In the early years of civilization there, most men shaved their heads bald while women braided their long hair into elaborate styles pinned to the top of their heads. They also covered their hair with netting, scarves, or turbans.

Elaborate hairstyles soon became important for both men and women in Mesopotamia. Men started to grow their hair longer and would wear it in waves. The king began to wear a full beard and long braided hair tied in a large bun at the nape of his neck. Women continued to wear their hair long, twisting it into large buns that covered the top of the head to the base of the neck and adorning it with ribbons and pins.

The wealthiest people decorated their elaborate hairstyles with beautifully made jewelry of gold and silver. A royal tomb from Sumeria dating from 2500 B.C.E. included a golden helmet with a leather lining. The gold of the helmet was expertly formed to resemble the hairstyle popular for men of the time: waves around the face with a bun tied in the back. The same tomb contained jewels of the queen as well. One of the most impressive pieces is a headdress made of a wreath of golden leaves and blue lapis lazuli flowers with a golden fan topped with similar flowers in the back. In addition to these ornate headdresses, the king and queen also wore beautiful jewelry.

Assyrian rule from 1380 to 612 B.C.E. altered hairstyles slightly. Men wore full beards and mustaches with longer curled hair. But some people with certain occupations, such as priests, doctors, and slaves, had specific hairstyles and headdresses, especially for special ceremonies. The king, for example, wore a tall hat made of alternating rows of patterned and plain bands topped with a pointed cone. Persians, who ruled Mesopotamia from 550 to 330 B.C.E., continued to curl their hair but began to wear rounded and pointed hats, probably made of leather.

FOR MORE INFORMATION

Payne, Blanche. *History of Costume: From the Ancient Egyptians to the Twentieth Century.* New York: Harper and Row, 1965.

Turbans

Sculpture showing a man wearing typical Mesopotamian turban.
Reproduced by permission of © Gianni Dagli Orti/CORBIS.

A turban—or hat made of elaborately wrapped, finely woven fabric—adorned the heads of women as early as the Sumerian civilization, which began in 3000 B.C.E. The Sumerians lived in the fertile valley between the Tigris and Euphrates Rivers in modern-day Iraq. Skilled weavers used their own hands and machines called looms to make the delicate, lightweight fabrics that turbans required. Sumerian sculptures, statues, and royal tomb remains depict women wearing turbans so elaborate that they must have required help in wrapping them. Sumerian turbans draped around women's heads in many different complex decorative ways. Turbans represented one of the many intricate styles for dressing hair that Sumerians practiced.

Though little is known about the earliest turbans

worn in Mesopotamia, the area in which the Sumerians lived, we do know that the turban became an important form of headwear for men in the Middle East, the Far East, and Africa for much of recorded history. They were common from the earliest years of civilization in India before the third century C.E., and they became popular among Turks after the decline of the Byzantine Empire in 1453 C.E. They are now worn by members of the Sikh religion, as well as by some Muslims and Hindus, in order to show their religious faith.

FOR MORE INFORMATION

Payne, Blanche. *History of Costume: From the Ancient Egyptians to the Twentieth Century.* New York: Harper and Row, 1965.

[*See also* **Volume 1, India: Turbans; Volume 2, Byzantine Empire: Turbans**]

Veils

In Mesopotamia, the region centered in present-day Iraq near the Tigris and Euphrates Rivers, a veil was a rectangular piece of cloth woven of linen, wool, or cotton and worn by women to hide their faces from public view. While the veils worn by the wealthiest women could be beautiful, veils were not worn for fashionable reasons alone. Veils were one of the first legally enforced garments.

The first use of the veil dates back to the Assyrians, the rulers of Mesopotamia from about 1380 to 612 B.C.E. The Assyrian empire stretched from the Persian Gulf to the Mediterranean Sea and reached into Egypt. Assyrian legal writings preserved on engraved stone tablets detail the first laws concerning the concealment of women's faces. The basis of these laws is found in the very different legal status of Assyrian men and women. Assyrian men enjoyed a great deal of power, while women had none. Women were considered property and legally belonged to their fathers until marriage, when ownership passed to their husbands. Assyrian laws about veils enforced the different status of men and women and also defined the differences between types of women.

Assyrian law dictated that wives, daughters, and widows must wear a veil, but prostitutes and slave women were forbidden from wearing a veil. The veil thus served as a way of protecting a father or husband's interest in his daughter or wife. The alluring face of a married or marriageable woman could not tempt men from beneath a veil. Wives, daughters, and widows would be severely punished for not covering their faces in public. But punishments also extended to male observers. If a man recognized a prostitute or slave woman wearing a veil and did not report her to an authority, he could be publicly flogged (beaten), mutilated (having his hand chopped off, for example), or imprisoned.

The tradition of veiling continues into the twenty-first century. The Muslim religion, which is practiced by millions of people across the globe, encourages the use of veils by women. Modern-day women who follow the Muslim religion customarily wear veils, and some countries, such as Saudi Arabia, have Muslim governments that enforce laws concerning women wearing veils.

FOR MORE INFORMATION

Nemet-Nejat, Karen Rhea. *Daily Life in Ancient Mesopotamia.* Westport, CT: Greenwood Press, 1998.

Payne, Blanche. *History of Costume: From the Ancient Egyptians to the Twentieth Century.* New York: Harper and Row, 1965.

Mesopotamian Body Decorations

Many different ethnic groups lived in Mesopotamia, the region between the Tigris and Euphrates Rivers in present-day Iraq, between 3000 B.C.E. and 300 B.C.E. Among the most prominent were the Sumerians, Akkadians, Babylonians, Assyrians, and Persians. Clothing historians have studied carved statues, the artifacts of royal tombs, and written tablets that show and describe the decorative accessories these people wore.

While slaves and the poorest people wore simple, functional clothes, the wealthiest could afford beautifully made jewelry. Men, women, and children all wore jewelry. A royal tomb from Sumeria dating from around 2500 B.C.E. included an abundance of beaded necklaces, rings, bracelets for the wrist and ankles, stickpins, and other jewelry. Made of gold and silver, the jewelry was set with decorative gemstones such as deep blue lapis lazuli, red carnelian, white alabaster, and sparkling crystals. Mesopotamian jewelry was large and elaborate. A pair of gold hoop earrings discovered in a queen's tomb, for example, are so large that they must have been worn hooked over the ears because they would have been too heavy to hang from the earlobes.

Little evidence remains about how the people of Mesopotamia groomed themselves, but the evidence that does exist indicates that Mesopotamians treated their bodies with great care. Sumerian texts include a story of a goddess bathing and perfuming herself for her bridegroom. To make perfume, Mesopotamians soaked fragrant plants in water and added oil. Some texts indicate that women wore makeup. Shells filled with pigments of red, white, yellow, blue, green, and black with carved ivory applicators have been found in tombs. Perfume was also important for cosmetic, medicinal, and other uses.

FOR MORE INFORMATION

Nemet-Nejat, Karen Rhea. *Daily Life in Ancient Mesopotamia.* Westport, CT: Greenwood Press, 1998.

Payne, Blanche, Geitel Winakor, and Jane Farrell-Beck. *The History of Costume.* 2nd ed. New York: HarperCollins, 1992.

Mesopotamian Footwear

As civilizations developed in Mesopotamia between 3000 and 300 B.C.E., foot coverings became more important. From the earliest times to about 911 B.C.E., the available evidence indicates that the people who lived in Mesopotamia, the region between the Tigris and Euphrates Rivers in present-day Iraq, went without any footwear at all. Even though these people had developed needles for sewing garments, looms for weaving, and the skills to make beautiful gold jewelry, they worked, entertained, worshiped, and went to

Working men often wore sandals to protect their feet against the elements. *Reproduced by permission of © Gianni Dagli Orti/CORBIS.*

war with unadorned bare feet. Statues of kings and queens in elaborately fringed outfits and carefully styled hair show these people without shoes.

The first depictions of people wearing foot coverings appear between 911 and 612 B.C.E. during the time of Assyrian rule. Although no samples of Assyrian footwear have been discovered, sculptures, statues, and bas-reliefs, or wall carvings, on the ruins of palace walls show men wearing sandals for some occasions, women in slippers with toe coverings, and warriors wearing boots with laces tied below the knee. Not until 550 to 330 B.C.E., when the Persians ruled, was footwear common. Regrettably, almost nothing is known about the details of how these shoes were made.

FOR MORE INFORMATION

Payne, Blanche, Geitel Winakor, and Jane Farrell-Beck. *The History of Costume.* 2nd ed. New York: HarperCollins, 1992.

Sandals

While the men living in the Sumerian (3000–2000 B.C.E.), the Akkadian (2350–2218 B.C.E.), and the Babylonian (1894–1595 B.C.E.) empires of Mesopotamia, the region between the Tigris and Euphrates Rivers in present-day Iraq, went barefoot all the time, Assyrian men began to wear sandals for everyday use around 911 B.C.E. Showing these changes are sculptures and bas-reliefs, or wall carvings, from the time period depicting men with foot coverings. The evidence suggests that all men went barefoot while worshipping and some men continued to go barefoot all the time. Some, however, began to wear protective sandals for everyday use, especially those living in the more mountainous areas, and some wore boots while fighting wars or hunting.

No Assyrian sandals have survived, but the remaining pictures and sculptures show that they had a wedge heel, a heel covering, and were held to the foot with straps and a toe ring. These sandals were probably made out of leather or strong grasses called reeds and are the earliest foot coverings in Mesopotamia.

FOR MORE INFORMATION

Payne, Blanche, Geitel Winakor, and Jane Farrell-Beck. *The History of Costume.* 2nd ed. New York: HarperCollins, 1992.

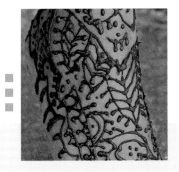

India

India is a vast subcontinent, or landmass that is part of a continent but is considered an independent entity, that contains many varied geographical regions. The Himalayan mountain range, which includes the highest mountains in the world, stretches across the north of the country along its border with Tibet. Three of India's largest rivers originate in the Himalayas: the Indus, the Ganges, and the Brahmaputra. These rivers feed a vast flat plain at the foothills of the Himalayas called the Indo-Gangetic Plain. A lush rainforest covers the northeast. These fertile lands are home to farmers. The west of India is covered by the Thar Desert, home to desert nomads, people with no permanent residence who move from place to place usually with the seasons. The southern tip of India is much drier and less fertile, while most people fish for a living along the western and eastern coasts.

Origins of Indian civilization

Indian civilization is based on the cultures of peoples as varied as the country's geography. The first Indians lived in the Indus Valley civilization that flourished along the Indus River in modern-day Pakistan, from 2500 to 1600 B.C.E. Remains from the Indus Valley civilization that have been recovered by archeologists, scientists who study the physical remains of ancient cultures, indicate that the society was quite advanced, with well-built brick houses, buildings for storing grain, paved roads, a written language, and a citadel, or a fortress from which a city is ruled and protected. These peoples, called Dravidians, were invaded by a nomadic tribe called Aryans who eventually settled throughout present-day northern India. The cultures of these two different societies combined and created the Hindu religion, which has been the dominant cultural

The Taj Mahal is one of the most well-known landmarks in India and an important cultural symbol. *Reproduced by permission of Ms. Susan D. Rock.*

force in India for thousands of years and heavily influenced the habits of dress practiced by Indians. The blending of various cultures has become the hallmark of Indian civilization up to the present day.

Over the years, nomadic tribes and other invading peoples have continued to shape Indian civilization. The Mauryan Empire, which flourished in 250 B.C.E. and dominated northern India for about 140 years, had a large army, complex tax system, and an organized government. After witnessing the brutality of war, Emperor Ashoka, the last Mauryan leader, converted to Buddhism, a religion that encourages people to be accepting of differences among them and to live together peacefully. Ashoka's peaceful teachings and kindness continue to influence life in India.

The second great empire in Indian history was the Gupta Empire, which lasted from 319 to 550 C.E. The Guptas encouraged learning, especially in the arts and sciences. Under Gupta rule the world was discovered to be round and the mathematical concept of zero came into being. Another great change in Indian life occurred from the eighth to the sixteenth century when Muslims slowly invaded India and eventually conquered it to create the Mogul Empire, which ruled all of India and other areas for approximately two hundred years, from about 1500 to 1700 C.E. The Muslims strongly influenced the peoples of India; many converted to the Muslim religion and began wearing clothes that conformed to the Muslim religion's dress code. The Moguls did tolerate other religions, and they created a peaceful advanced society that fostered the arts and sciences.

Trading brings more change

Over the years the rulers of India nurtured the skills of many craftsmen. These craftsmen learned to create beautiful jewelry, weave fine cotton fabric and other more expensive materials, develop intricate dyeing and decorating practices to beautify fabric, and excel at making other products for trade, such as spices and tea. By 1498, when Portuguese explorer Vasco da Gama (c. 1460–1524) reached India, Indian civilization had a great deal to offer other cultures. Europeans desired Indian spices and fabrics in particular. The East India Company of Britain controlled most of the trading in India by the 1600s. When the Mogul Empire ended and India was divided into many small kingdoms in 1700, trade with Europe did not stop. In fact, Britain continued to gain power in the region and by 1858 India had become a British colony.

Although Indians benefited from new railways, roads, and postal and telegraph services under British rule, living under British control frustrated many Indians. By the twentieth century many wanted to rule themselves. Mahatma Gandhi (1869–1948) inspired Indians to peacefully extract control of India from the British. India became an independent democracy in 1947 and was now the seventh-largest country in the world. At that time the Hindu majority dominated India and the Muslim minority created the countries of Pakistan and Bangladesh.

Modern-day India

India continues to be home to very diverse peoples. Most people follow the Hindu religion; about 10 percent are Muslim; others are Buddhists, Christians, Jews, and other religions. India recognizes fifteen official languages, but nearly one thousand different dialects are spoken in the country. Indian society had been divided into four distinct social groups, called castes, since 1500 B.C.E. These castes were based on people's jobs: priests were considered the highest, most respected class, followed by warriors and princes, and then by merchants and farmers. The lowest caste was made up of people called the "untouchables," those who worked with sewage or garbage, among other "unclean" things. The caste system locked people into a certain position in society for life. If a person married outside of his or her caste, he or she would risk being shunned by family and friends. The Indian government outlawed the caste system in 1949 and has instituted policies to make up for the discrimination of the caste system's rules.

Although Indian culture has felt the effects of many outside influences, its distinctive costume traditions have lasted for thousands of years. The clothing styles worn from the earliest civilizations in India continue to be worn in modern times. The garments made in ancient India were woven of light fabric and wrapped around the body to create different styles. Although Indians knew how to sew before the Muslims invaded, it was Muslims who popularized the wearing of sewn garments, including trousers and jackets. Of course trade with the West also opened India to the cultures of Europe, and many modern-day Indians do wear clothes similar to Westerners, especially men working in Indian cities. Yet styles of thousands of years ago continue to influence Indian fashion to this day.

FOR MORE INFORMATION

Cifarelli, Megan. *India: One Nation, Many Traditions.* New York: Benchmark Books, 1996.

"Excerpts: Evolution of Court Costume." *ritukumar.com.* http://www.ritukumar.com/ancient.htm (accessed on July 24, 2003).

"A Historical Outline." *fashionindia.net.* http://www.fashionindia.net/history_fashion/history_fashion.htm (accessed on July 24, 2003).

Kalman, Bobbie. *India: The People.* New York: Crabtree Publishing, 1990.

Watson, Francis, with Dilip Hiro. *India: A Concise History.* New York: Thames and Hudson, 2002.

Indian Clothing

A historical record of Indian clothing is difficult to trace. While there is an abundance of sculpture and literature dating from the earliest periods of civilization in the Indus Valley (which flourished along the Indus River in modern-day Pakistan) around 2500 B.C.E., scholars have had difficulty dating the changes in clothing styles and naming the variations on certain styles over time. Another problem in identifying trends in Indian clothing is the abundance of different ethnic and cultural groups that have lived and are living in the country; each of which has its own distinctive style. These circumstances make it possible to make generalizations about Indian clothing, but not to make concrete statements about each and every style worn in the country.

The oldest type of Indian clothing was fashioned out of yards of unsewn fabric that were then wound around the body in a variety of ways to create different, distinct garments. This clothing was woven most commonly out of cotton but could also be made of goat hair, linen, silk, or wool. Some of the most popular garments are a wrapped dress called a sari, a pair of pants called a dhoti, a hat called a turban, and a variety of scarves. These styles of garments have been popular in India since the beginning of its civilization and continue to be worn in the twenty-first century.

Changes in the styles worn by Indians reflected their contact with other peoples. As different tribes of people invaded or entered

An Indian women often has to keep almost her entire body covered in clothing. *Reproduced by permission of © Michael Maslan Historic Photographs/CORBIS.*

India to trade or to live, they brought with them distinctive clothing styles. Throughout the different regions of India, the changes in clothing styles can be linked to some contact with other cultures. For example, Indians knew how to sew long before the sixteenth century when the Moguls, or Muslims, invaded, and they had long adorned their wrapped garments with elaborate embroidery stitches. But when the Moguls took power over the region, the Moguls' style of sewn clothing became popular among Indians. Sewn jackets and trousers were among the styles popularized by the Mogul leaders, although traditional wrapped clothing remained common.

Trade contacts also spread Indian clothing styles and cloth to other parts of the world. The Dutch and the English established trade routes with India in the late 1400s, and by the 1600s Indian cotton was exported to regions throughout Europe and the American colonies, where shawls made of Indian cloth became especially popular. In the twenty-first century India continues to be a major source of finely woven fabrics for garment manufacturers worldwide.

FOR MORE INFORMATION

Askari, Nasreen, and Liz Arthur. *Uncut Cloth: Saris, Shawls, and Sashes.* London, England: Merrell Holbertson, 1999.

"Excerpts: Evolution of Court Costume." *ritukumar.com.* http://www. ritukumar.com/ancient.htm (accessed on July 24, 2003).

Goswamy, B. N., and Kalyan Krishna. *Indian Costume in the Collection of the Calico Museum of Textiles.* Ahmedabad, India: D. S. Mehta, 1993.

"A Historical Outline." *fashionindia.net.* http://www.fashionindia.net/history _fashion/history_fashion.htm (accessed on July 24, 2003).

Burka

A long, flowing garment that covers the whole body from head to feet, the burka, also known as burqa or abaya, is an important part of the dress of Muslim women in many different countries. Some burkas leave the face uncovered, but most have a cloth or metal grid that hides the face from view while allowing the wearer to see. The exact origin of the burka is unknown, but similar forms of veiling have been worn by women in countries such as India, Pakistan, Saudi Arabia, and Afghanistan since the beginning of the Muslim religion in 622 C.E.

The Koran, the holy book of Islam, directs believers to cover themselves and be humble before God. Different societies and religious leaders have interpreted this command of the Koran in many different ways, often requiring both men and women to cover their heads as a sign of religious respect. Some Muslim societies have required women to cover themselves more modestly than men, covering not only their heads but also most of their bodies and even their faces. The burka is one example of very modest clothing worn by Muslim women.

The burka has mainly been worn in very conservative Muslim cultures, which often restrict the movement and power of women. Young girls are not required to cover themselves with a burka, but at puberty or marriage they begin to wear it. While women do not wear the burka while they are home with their families, they are required to wear it when they are in public or in the presence of men who are not family members. In many places the burka was first worn as a sign of wealth and leisure, because a woman could not easily work while wearing the long garment.

Though the burka often appears confining and limiting to Western eyes, many devout Muslim women choose to wear the long veil. Some say that the coverage of the burka gives them a privacy that actually makes them feel freer to move about in society. However, others say that even though the burka protects women from the staring eyes of strange men, it does not prevent the wearer from being touched or pinched by passing men. Also, many Muslim women who live in very conservative societies are forced to wear the burka whether they want to or not, and many have been punished harshly for refusing to cover themselves as their authorities demand.

Two women wear white burkas, traditional women's dress in cultures of the Middle East. *Reproduced by permission of © Bettmann/CORBIS.*

FOR MORE INFORMATION

El Guindi, Fadwa. *Veil: Modesty, Privacy, and Resistance.* New York: Berg, 1999.

Murtaza, Mutahhari. *The Islamic Modest Dress.* Chicago: Kazi Publications, 1992.

[*See also* **Volume 1, Mesopotamia: Veils**]

Chadar

This man wears a heavy brown wool chadar over his shoulders and arms, most likely for warmth. *Reproduced by permission of © Lindsay Hebberd/CORBIS.*

The chadar, also spelled chador or chadoor, is a multipurpose garment worn by many people in India since before the third century C.E. Indians and others living in countries of the Middle East continue to wear the chadar to this day. Though the size, shape, and color of the chadar vary somewhat in different cultures, it is basically a large scarf, about three yards long and one yard wide, or larger. Both men and women use the chadar as a shawl or wrap for protection from the weather, for modesty, and for religious purposes. Some chadars have decorative or fringed edges.

The chadar is a common accessory in desert countries like Afghanistan, where it is often wrapped around the body, head, and face for protection from sand and dust storms. In less harsh weather, men usually wear the chadar around the shoulders, like a shawl. Women in Muslim societies are often required to cover themselves more modestly than men, and they wear the chadar over their heads as well, holding an end between their teeth when they wish to cover their faces. Some women wrap the chadar tightly around their neck and head to form a sort of headdress that may cover all or part of the face. The abundant fabric of the chadar is useful for many purposes. A mother may wrap her baby in one end of the scarf and use it to cover them both while she breastfeeds. Ends of the chadar may also be used to tie small bundles to make them easy to carry. Some women's chadars are large enough to cover the wearer from head to toe, similar to the long burka also worn by Muslim women.

The chadar also has religious and ceremonial purposes. The color and designs used in the fabric often have religious significance. Many Muslim men use the chadar to wrap themselves or kneel upon it for prayer, and a large version is often used to wrap around the dead before burial.

FOR MORE INFORMATION

El Guindi, Fadwa. *Veil: Modesty, Privacy, and Resistance.* New York: Berg, 1999.

Murtaza, Mutahhari. *The Islamic Modest Dress.* Chicago: Kazi Publications, 1992.

Choli

At the dawn of Indian civilization in 2500 B.C.E., women left their breasts bare. It was under Muslim rule, which lasted from 1500 to 1700 C.E., that women began to dress more modestly. The choli, a sewn garment that covered women's breasts, became popular as the Muslims rose in power. The choli is worn with a skirt or under a sari, a draped dress.

Although Indian women wore unstitched garments from the beginning of Indian civilization, from the first invasion of the Muslims in about the tenth century some Indians began to wear stitched garments. The choli is such a garment. The first choli only covered a woman's breasts, leaving her back bare. The garment evolved into many different variations, the most common being a tight-fitting bodice with short or long sleeves that ended just below the breasts or just above the waist. Many other variations of the choli are worn throughout India today and include styles fastened with ties, versions with rounded necklines, and some that shape or flatten the breasts.

Two young girls wear several items of traditional Indian dress, including brightly colored cholis. *Reproduced by permission of © Howard Davies/CORBIS.*

Worn mostly in the north and west of India, the choli is distinguished in different regions by various decorations. The fabric can be dyed bright colors, embroidered, or appliquéd with mirrors. Cholis are made of cotton or silk but can also be made of organza and brocade for special occasions.

FOR MORE INFORMATION

Goswamy, B. N., and Kalyan Krishna. *Indian Costume in the Collection of the Calico Museum of Textiles.* Ahmedabad, India: D. S. Mehta, 1993.

Dhoti and Lungi

Two styles of clothing have been most popular with Indian men and boys from ancient times to the present day: the dhoti and the lungi. Both the dhoti and the lungi are garments made from wrapping unsewn cloth around the waist to cover the loins and most of the legs of their wearers. Although these garments are most often worn by men, women do wear them and other similar garments that resemble skirts.

A dhoti is a large cloth wrapped around the waist and then between the legs with the end tucked into the fabric at the waist in back. A dhoti resembles trousers but is made of unsewn fabric. Commonly, dhoti drape below the wearer's knees to mid calf, but some men in warmer parts of India and young boys wear the dhoti above the knee. Although normally created out of a single piece of fabric, the dhoti can also be secured by a kamarband, or a piece of cloth tied around the waist like a belt. The lungi also covers the man from the waist down but resembles a long skirt. A lungi is made by wrapping a cloth around the waist and securing it with a knot called a duba. Both the dhoti and the lungi can be worn alone with a bare chest or with a variety of upper body coverings including shawls, shirts, or jackets.

This man wears a lungi with a colorful pattern around his legs and waist. *Reproduced by permission of © Sheldan Collins/CORBIS.*

Both dhoti and lungi have been woven out of silk, cotton, and sometimes wool. Although the dhoti is most commonly made of thin white cotton, the lungi is often dyed bright colors or decorated with colorful patterns. Lungis are either dyed a plain color or decorated with stripes or plaids and bordered in a contrasting color. If the garment is made with dyed yarn, the fabric is most often woven with a pattern of two colors. Popular colors for everyday lungis include white, dark red, blue, brown, and black while those worn for ceremonies or festive occasions are made in brighter shades of yellow, pink, turquoise, dark blue, green, and purple. Other decorations include embroidery on the borders, appliquéd mirrors, and patterns made from tie-dyeing or stamping carved blocks.

In ancient times entire families would be involved in spinning and dyeing the yarn used and weaving the fabric for these garments. Mahatma Gandhi (1869-1948), the leader who rallied Indians in nonviolent protest against British rule in the early 1900s, encouraged Indians to shun imported British fabrics and to weave their clothes at home. Some Indians continue to weave fabric at home, but large factories with power looms are responsible for the greatest portion of modern-day production.

FOR MORE INFORMATION

Askari, Nasreen, and Liz Arthur. *Uncut Cloth: Saris, Shawls, and Sashes.* London, England: Merrell Holbertson, 1999.

Jama

The jama is a jacket that was worn by men in India following its introduction by Mogul, or Muslim, invaders in the sixteenth century C.E., and which influenced later menswear. The jama resembles sewn jackets worn in ancient Persia, modern-day Iran. The jama is identified by its long sleeves, tight-fitting chest, or bodice, tie closures at the side, and flared skirt. While the sleeves and chest are similar in the many variations of the jama, the jacket closures and the length and flare of the skirt have changed over time. Early versions of the jama, for example, had skirts that reached to mid thigh and flared slightly at the ends. By the eighteenth century, however, jama had long flowing skirts that touched the floor. The jacket tie closures were modified by the different religious groups in India. Muslims tied the jama at the right armpit from the sixteenth century forward, while Hindus tied their jamas on the left. Mogul rulers insisted that Hindus and Muslims continued this custom in order to distinguish themselves from each other.

The jama is the forerunner of other jackets that became popular in India. The influence of British styles in the eighteenth century pushed the jama out of fashion. The jacket was replaced by the angarkha and the choga, which were both gradually replaced by the chapkanm, achkan, and shervani in the nineteenth century. These later styles of jacket were slim fitting and closed with buttons.

FOR MORE INFORMATION

Goswamy, B. N., and Kalyan Krishna. *Indian Costume in the Collection of the Calico Museum of Textiles.* Ahmedabad, India: D. S. Mehta, 1993.

Kumar, Ritu. *Costumes and Textiles of Royal India.* London, England: Christies Books, 1999.

[*See also* **Volume 5, 1961–79: Nehru Jacket**]

Punjabi Suit

The Punjabi suit, also known as the salwar kameez, is an outfit worn primarily by Indian women but also by some men. The Punjabi suit became popular around the time of the Mogul Empire, from 1500 to 1700 C.E., and has continued to be worn by modern Indians to the present day. The Punjabi suit consists of a sleeved tunic-like

An Indian official wearing a plain Punjabi suit. *Reproduced by permission of © Bettmann/CORBIS.*

top that hangs to mid thigh and loose trousers that become narrow at the ankle. A scarf, or dupatta, is often draped around the neck as an accompaniment to the suit. Made of a variety of light fabrics, such as cotton and silk, the Punjabi suit can be plain but is more often decorated with printed fabric or embroidery. The decorations found on the garment are highly symbolic, often designed to guard against evil spirits that might harm the wearer.

FOR MORE INFORMATION

Goswamy, B. N., and Kalyan Krishna. *Indian Costume in the Collection of the Calico Museum of Textiles.* Ahmedabad, India: D. S. Mehta, 1993.

Purdah

The word "purdah" comes from the Hindu word meaning curtain or veil. Purdah is a complex set of rules, followed in some Muslim and Hindu societies, which restrict a woman's movements both in the outside world and within her own home. Meant to separate the family as a unit from those outside the family, purdah requires a woman to isolate herself from those who are not in her immediate family by veiling her body and face or sitting behind screens or curtains. The custom of purdah originated among the Assyrians and the Persians, peoples who inhabited ancient Mesopotamia, the region between the Tigris and Euphrates Rivers in present-day Iraq, around 1000 B.C.E. The term purdah is also sometimes used to describe the heavy veiling that women wear under the rules of purdah.

As early as the 2000s B.C.E., ancient Babylonian men had strict rules about the movements of women, requiring them to cover their bodies and faces and to be accompanied by a male chaperone when in public. A few centuries later, Assyrian and Persian men refined these rules further, insisting that women remain inside their homes most of the time, concealed from view behind curtains. When the Arab people conquered the Persians during the seventh century B.C.E., they adopted many of the Persian customs including the seclusion of women. They blended this custom with their Muslim religion, and many Muslim societies began to practice some form

MODERN ISLAMIC DRESS

Islamic dress, also called hijab, or veiling, is worn by Muslims in modern Islamic countries and by many Muslims who live in countries that are not primarily Islamic. Developed from statements found in the Islamic holy book, the Koran, the rules of Muslim dress mainly call for modesty and simplicity in clothes. In general, Islamic dress consists of loose clothing that covers the body and the head, but there is no one type of clothing for all Muslim people. Some governments, religious leaders, and sects of Islam often have very strict modesty requirements. At the same time, in urban areas, such as Cairo, the capital of Egypt, the standards of modest dress are often looser, allowing for more Western styles of clothing. However, most devout Muslims try to follow some version of the rules of modesty first laid down in the words of the Koran and by the prophet Muhammad (c. 570–632), founder of Islam.

The rules of modesty are somewhat different for women than for men. Both are required to wear loose clothing that does not cling and reveal the shape of the body. However, while it is believed that Muhammad ordered women to cover all of their bodies except the face and hands, men were only commanded to cover the area between their navel and their knees. However, in most modern Islamic societies men are expected to cover their legs and arms, just as women are. Men were also forbidden to wear silk and gold, while women were allowed to wear them. Since part of modesty is not showing off one's wealth, Islamic dress is not ornate or expensively decorated, but clothing is usually simple and little jewelry or makeup is worn. Modesty also means not displaying pride or vanity about one's lack of wealth, so ragged clothes are also frowned upon by the rules of Islamic dress.

In a modern urban society, such as that of many Middle Eastern cities, women's Islamic dress usually consists of a skirt that reaches the ankles, a long-sleeved shirt, and a headscarf, also called a hijab. Some women may wear a Western-style jacket over their blouse, and many wear slacks or jeans with a long-sleeved shirt and hijab. Muslim men in cities also usually wear long pants and long-sleeved shirts, much the same way most Western men do. It is generally considered unacceptable for men to wear shorts or go shirtless. In rural areas, and in some conservative countries like Iran in the 1980s and Afghanistan in the 1990s, dress rules have often been stricter. Women may be required to cover their faces as well as their heads, and men may wear ankle-length, loose robes called galabiyyas. In some areas men also cover their heads with scarves or turbans.

Though some in the West assume that Muslim women must be forced to veil themselves and obey the rules of Islamic dress, many Muslim women see things quite differently. To them, Islamic dress represents an Arab and Muslim identity in which they take great pride. They may feel safer both on the streets and in the workplace because their style of dress, which shows their religious devotion, makes it less likely that men will bother them. In nations like Egypt, which do not have religious governments but do have religious political parties, wearing Islamic dress can also make a political statement. On the other hand, there are women who rebel against the rules of Islamic dress and maintain they have a right to dress as they wish.

In countries that are not primarily Muslim, Muslim women who follow the rules of Islamic dress may be treated differently than non-Muslim women. People of different religions sometimes do not understand the rules of Islam and make assumptions about the political beliefs or lifestyle of women who wear a headscarf or men who wear a turban. Some Muslim women have even removed their headscarf in order to apply for jobs because they feel employers would be less likely to hire them in Islamic dress.

of purdah. The influence spread across India as well, and many people of the Hindu religion also began to practice purdah.

In the twenty-first century strict purdah is mainly practiced in rural areas of India, Pakistan, Bangladesh, and some other countries that practice the Muslim or Hindu religions. The rules of purdah usually apply only to women after they are married, and they vary somewhat between Muslim and Hindu peoples. For the Hindus, purdah is a tool for defining the family, as well as showing modesty. Young married women mainly associate with members of their own family. They rarely travel, seldom go out in public, and are always completely veiled when they do. Even at home, they only show their faces to members of the family they grew up in and to their husbands, covering their faces or remaining behind a screen even around their in-laws. Though they may talk to women and children outside their immediate families through the veil, they usually do not speak to any men outside their own birth families. As these women grow older, the rules of purdah relax and many go unveiled inside their homes.

In Muslim families the rules of purdah are less strict and do not apply to family members of the wife or husband. Muslim purdah is meant mainly to ensure modesty of dress and behavior and to separate women from men who are not related by blood or marriage.

Many women have rebelled against the restrictions of purdah, saying that the confining rules limit their access to education and information about the world. Those who support the practice say that purdah is meant to improve women's position and increase respect for them by freeing them from concern about their appearance and from men's reactions to their bodies. However, as many people in Muslim and Hindu societies have become more educated and many Muslim women have become more ambitious and independent, the practice of purdah has begun to disappear.

FOR MORE INFORMATION

Ahmed, Leila. *Women and Gender in Islam: Historical Roots of a Modern Debate*. New Haven, CT: Yale University Press, 1992.

Black, J. Anderson, and Madge Garland. Updated and revised by Frances Kennett. *A History of Fashion*. New York: William Morrow, 1980.

Brooks, Geraldine. *Nine Parts of Desire: The Hidden World of Islamic Women*. New York: Anchor Books, 1995.

El Guindi, Fadwa. *Veil: Modesty, Privacy, and Resistance.* New York: Berg, 1999.

Murtaza, Mutahhari. *The Islamic Modest Dress.* Chicago: Kazi Publications, 1992.

[*See also* **Volume 1, Mesopotamia: Veils; Volume 1, India: Burka**]

Sari

The sari, sometimes spelled saree, is a draped dress, created from a single piece of fabric five to nine yards long, which is wrapped around a woman's body in a variety of ways. The resulting garment can be practical working attire or an elegant ceremonial gown, depending on the type of fabric used and the style of draping. While women wear the sari, men wear a version of the wrapped garment called a dhoti. A daily garment worn by approximately 75 percent of the female population of India during the twenty-first century, the sari is one of the oldest known items of clothing that is still in use. Saris were mentioned in the Vedas, the ancient sacred literature of the Hindu religion, which has been dated back to 3000 B.C.E., and many people believe that saris may have been worn even earlier.

Like the Greeks and Romans who followed them, the ancient people of India mainly wore garments that were wrapped and draped, rather than sewn. This was not because they did not know the art of sewing—early Indian people were experts in fine weaving and embroidery—but because they preferred the flexibility and creativity that draped clothing allowed. Loose, flowing garments were practical in the hot climate of southern Asia, and the sari, woven of cotton or silk, was both cool and graceful. Though rich and poor alike wore the sari, the wealthy could afford to have fine silk fabric with costly decorations, while the poor might wear rough plain cotton.

The basic wrap of a sari usually involves winding it around the waist first then wrapping it around the upper body. Women frequently wear underclothes of a half-slip tied around the waist and a tight blouse or breast-wrap that ends just below the bust,

A young girl wearing a sari. Saris are usually elaborately wrapped around the body, as shown here. *Reproduced by permission of © Brian A. Vikander/CORBIS.*

which provide the basis for wrapping the fabric of the sari. There are many different styles of wrapping and draping the sari, and these vary according to gender, region, social class, ethnic background, and personal style. Instead of wrapping the fabric around the chest, the ends of the sari can be simply thrown over one or both shoulders. Sometimes an end is pulled between the legs and tucked into the back of the skirt, making it into loose pants, which are practical for working. Many men wear saris that only cover the lower half of their bodies. Though saris are usually wrapped to the left, people from some regions of India favor wrapping to the right. When the abundant material of the sari is wrapped around the waist, it is usually pleated to create graceful folds and drapes. The number of pleats and the direction they fold can vary and is sometimes dictated by religious belief. Though many modern saris are mass-produced, saris made of handwoven cloth are important to many people as a political symbol of Indian pride.

Though many Indian people, both those living in India and those who live in other countries, have adopted Western dress, it is very common for Indian women to wear the sari for important ceremonies, such as weddings.

FOR MORE INFORMATION

Chishti, Rta Kapur, and Amba Sanyal. *Saris of India.* Seattle, WA: University of Washington Press, 1991.

Lynton, Linda. *The Sari: Styles, Patterns, History, Techniques.* New York: W. W. Norton, 2002.

[*See also* **Volume 1, India: Dhoti and Lungi**]

Uttariya

Both men and women covered their upper bodies in ancient India with a garment called an uttariya. An uttariya was an unsewn cloth or scarf. Made commonly of cotton, the uttariya could also be made of animal skin, linen, or—for the wealthiest people—silk. Some writings from early India, written in the ancient Sanskrit language, refer to garments being made of the bark of the tree of paradise or the filaments of lotus flowers. The uttariya always accompanied other garments. Men wore them with a type of wrapped garment called a dhoti, and women wore them with a sari or an antariya, a wrap around the lower body.

No matter the fabric, uttariyas were light and delicate because of India's warm climate. The delicate material used for uttariyas did not last long, and no examples of the actual early garments have survived for historians to study. Costume historians must rely on the depictions of the ancient form of the garments on existing sculptures and in remaining literature.

Uttariyas could be draped over the left shoulder to cover the chest, thrown loosely over the shoulders, tied in place across the wearer's back, or held by a belt at the waist. Although men wore the uttariya to cover their upper bodies from the earliest years of Indian civilization, women did not typically cover their upper bodies until the fourth century C.E. At that time the uttariya became an important garment to preserve the modesty of women. Women would use the uttariya to cover their breasts in public, and some began to use a portion of their uttariya as a veil to cover their heads.

Uttariyas could be made of the simplest, plain cloth for those of modest income. But wealthy Indians often wore highly decorated uttariyas made of brightly dyed cloth of red, blue, or gold, among other colors. The uttariyas of the wealthy were also adorned with studs of pearls and other jewels, embroidery, and painted designs.

Like the dhoti, the sari, and the turban, the uttariya remains one of the garments from ancient times that is still worn in modern India.

FOR MORE INFORMATION

Goswamy, B. N., and Kalyan Krishna. *Indian Costume in the Collection of the Calico Museum of Textiles.* Ahmedabad, India: D. S. Mehta, 1993.

Mohapatra, R. P. *Fashion Styles of Ancient India: A Study of Kalinga from Earliest Times to Sixteenth Century A.D.* Delhi, India: B. R. Publishing, 1992.

Indian Headwear

Over thousands of years, Indians perfected the art of looping, knotting, and twisting fabric into elaborate and elegant outfits. They applied similar techniques to their hair, twisting and tying their hair into a variety of styles too numerous to count. Hair arrangement became an art form in India. Terra-cotta, or clay, figurines and sculptures from the Indus Valley civilization dating back as far as 2500 B.C.E. depict intricate hairstyles for both men and women that reveal differences between regions and time periods. Literature from the earliest times in India also describes the importance of hairstyles.

Having long, clean, untangled hair was important to Indians. From the earliest years of Indian civilization, both men and women wore their hair long. Indians took great pride in caring for their hair. Shampooed with a type of juice and dried in the sun, hair was scented with fragrant flowers, herbs, spices, or oils. To style their hair perfectly, Indians used mirrors and combs.

In general, the hair of both men and women was combed upward into a large bun and held in place on top of the head with a cord. But this generalization reflects only the basic shape of the styled hair. The variety of styles found on sculptures is astounding and includes corkscrew curls, ponytails, chignons (a knot of hair tied at the back of the head), long single braids, and even hairstyles with rows of upturned curls piled on top of the head that made it look like a tower of flames.

To hold hair in place, Indians coated their hair with bee's wax, castor oil, and other sticky substances, or used ornaments. While the sticky substances could hold hair in styles as different as large cone-shaped buns and tight forehead curls, ornaments added sparkle as well as held the hair in place. Indian hair ornaments were as simple as an unadorned cord or as elaborate as an expertly crafted golden crown.

Ribbons and strings of pearls, golden hairpins, forehead ornaments, nets, jeweled medallions, and clips are a few of the decorative accessories Indians added to their hair. Typically Indians wore several types of ornaments together. Tied with a cord on top of the head, hair could be styled with a series of pearl strings or ribbons and secured with a medallion. Then a forehead ornament could be attached.

Shaving was practiced in ancient Indian society. Most men used razor blades to shave their faces clean, although some religious men did wear full beards and long mustaches. Few men shaved their entire head bald. Those with clean-shaven heads were usually religious teachers or students. Aside from shaving all the hair off the head, some would leave a tuft of hair for tying into a knot. Fragrant flowers were occasionally secured in this knot.

Although some practices changed in India after Muslim civilizations began invading the mostly Hindu-dominated region in the sixteenth century C.E., hair care remained important in Indian society into the twenty-first century. Modern Indians wear their hair styled in traditional ways, such as a long single braid for women, or in styles that reflect the influence of Western culture, such as a short, cropped cut for men.

FOR MORE INFORMATION

Mohapatra, R. P. *Fashion Styles of Ancient India: A Study of Kalinga from Earliest Times to Sixteenth Century A.D.* Delhi, India: B. R. Publishing, 1992.

Turbans

From ancient times until the present day, the most common headwear for Indian men has been a turban. A turban is a length of cloth wrapped in a specific way around the top of the head. Most commonly worn outdoors, turbans can also be worn indoors.

Woven of cotton, silk, or wool, turbans can be simple or very ornate. The type of fabric, patterns or colors on the fabric, length of fabric, and wrapping technique used for the turban indicate the wearer's social status, religion, ethnicity, and, in some cases, profes-

sion. Followers of the Sikh religion, a religion based on the belief of one God and many paths, for example, are required to wear a starched muslin, or cotton cloth, turban made from a cloth about five or six meters in length. (Sikh men never cut their hair out of respect for it as God's creation and wrap it in these turbans.) In some regions, Sikhs wear white turbans while in others dark blue turbans are worn. Turbans worn in different regions of the Rajasthan Desert include the leheriya, or wave, a patterned turban that is worn especially during the monsoon season; the panchrang, or five-color, turban worn for celebrations; and the more simply designed bundi, or small dot patterned, and mothro, or small square patterned, turbans worn for serious, somber occasions.

Turbans can be decorated in a variety of ways. Often the fabric is dyed one color and bordered with a contrasting color. For more intricate designs, everyday turbans are block-printed or tie-dyed. Festive turbans or those worn by wealthier men are made of more expensive fabrics, such as silk, and even woven or stamped with gold thread.

Indian men wear turbans in a variety of different colors but they are often wrapped in the same way. *Reproduced by permission of AP/Wide World Photos.*

In most parts of India turbans are worn wrapped directly around the bare head of the wearer. However, in modern-day Pakistan and especially the areas near Iran, Afghanistan, and central Asia, turbans are wrapped over the top of a soft cap called a topi or a rigid cap covered with embroidery called a kulah.

There are many different styles of wrapping turbans. Two common ways include one continuous swirl around the head to form the turban or twisting the fabric into two parts and securing one end as a band around the forehead and then arranging the two segments into a diagonal tie on top of the head. Some wearers leave one end of the turban fabric hanging for decoration or for use as a head towel.

Turbans continue to be worn by men throughout India and by many Sikhs and Muslims throughout the world. The style is also worn by women in some cultures, such as the nomadic group known as Kurds living in parts of Syria, Iraq, and Turkey. A prewrapped version of the turban became a popular hat with European and American women in the 1960s. Some older women continue to wear it in their homes as a casual covering for hair rolled in curlers.

FOR MORE INFORMATION

Askari, Nasreen, and Liz Arthur. *Uncut Cloth: Saris, Shawls, and Sashes.* London, England: Merrell Holbertson, 1999.

Indian Body Decorations

Decorating and accessorizing the body plays an important part in ceremonial as well as everyday life in India, today as well as in the past. Sculptures trace the history of body decoration to the earliest civilizations in the Indus Valley, which flourished along the Indus River in modern-day Pakistan. Literature and paintings also document Indian body adornment traditions, many of which have been practiced in some form since 2500 B.C.E.

Indians use colors and patterns of makeup for various purposes. Married women signal their marital status by dyeing the center parting of their hair red. Mothers protect their babies from evil spirits by tracing their babies' eyes in black makeup and adding black decorations to their face. The color black is thought to repel harm from the delicate openings on the face. The many religious groups in India use makeup for religious purposes as well. Followers of several different religions indicate their religious devotions by wearing certain colors and patterns on their foreheads. For their wedding day, Hindu Indian women lighten their skin with rice powder, paint their face with red and black patterns, and redden the palms of their hands and the soles of their feet with henna, a reddish powder or paste made from the dried leaves of the henna bush.

Jewelry is another important decorative accessory in India. For as long as people have lived in the Indus Valley, Indians have worn beautiful rings, necklaces, and bracelets to adorn their bodies. Made of gold, silver, and bronze, decorated with carving, and imbedded with precious stones, jewelry serves to beautify all people, but especially women. Special jewelry is made to decorate every part of a woman's body, from the top of her forehead to the tips of her toes. Foreheads are draped with pearl strings; ears are pierced with long golden earrings; nostrils are pierced with studded gems; wrists and ankles are circled with jangling bracelets; and fingers and toes have rings.

Although modern Indian women who live in large cities may dress in Western styles during the twenty-first century, traditional styles of body decoration continue to be practiced in rural areas and for ceremonial occasions such as weddings.

FOR MORE INFORMATION

Gröning, Karl. *Body Decoration: A World Survey of Body Art.* Munich, Germany: Vendome Press, 1997.

Mohapatra, R. P. *Fashion Styles of Ancient India: A Study of Kalinga from Earliest Times to Sixteenth Century A.D.* Delhi, India: B. R. Publishing, 1992.

Foot Decorating

A foot decorated with henna, a reddish powder or paste. *Reproduced by permission of © Jeremy Horner/CORBIS.*

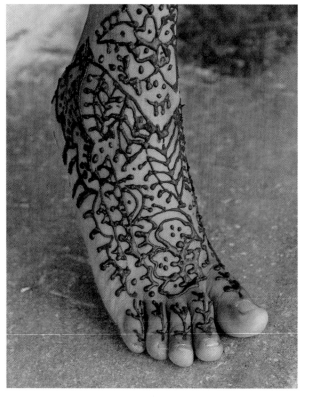

The foot has had religious and social significance in India since ancient times. Deities are represented by a set of divine footprints on items ranging from paintings and woven shawls to amulets—ornaments that are worn to protect the wearer. The feet of older people are revered by youth, lovers show their affection for each other by caressing each other's feet, and Indian mothers take special care of their babies' feet by massaging them. Indians have decorated their feet since the first Indus Valley civilization—which flourished along the Indus River in modern-day Pakistan—in 2500 B.C.E.

Men, women, and children in India all wear anklets. Anklets are not only decorative but meaningful. In the past, rulers often rewarded noblemen, landlords, or local officials with a present of a valuable anklet. And women in some regions of India wore anklets to show their marital status. Today, there remain many different varieties of anklets worn throughout India. The anklets of common people are mostly made of silver or brass, but the wealthy wear gold anklets studded with jewels.

While men and women wear anklets, usually only women's feet are decorated in their entirety. Women dye the soles of their feet red and, especially for their wedding day, have intricate designs of mehndi, or traditional henna stains, applied to the tops of their feet. Some women tattoo designs of fish, scorpions, or peacocks, which have special erotic meanings, on the tops of their feet and other parts of their body. In addition to several anklets, women also wear foot ornaments that decorate the tops of their feet and several toe rings that are sometimes connected to anklets by decorative chains. Foot decoration among Indian women remains so important in Indian culture that many women, with the exception of those living in modern cities, continue to go barefoot quite often.

FOR MORE INFORMATION

Jain-Neubauer, Jutta. *Feet and Footwear in Indian Culture.* Toronto, Canada: Bata Shoe Museum, 2000.

[*See also* **Volume 1, India: Henna Stains; Volume 1, India: Jewelry**]

Forehead Markings

Many people of India, especially those who follow the Hindu religion, wear colored markings on their foreheads and other parts of their bodies. In general, forehead markings identify a person's third eye, or what Hindus believe is the center of a person's nervous system, the area in which a person can see spiritual truths. These markings usually take the form of red, white, and black dots or lines, or combinations of dots and lines, which have either social or religious meanings. The practice of marking the body, especially the forehead, with these symbols dates back to ancient people who lived in southern Asia around 2500 B.C.E.

Many historians believe that ancient ancestors of the modern residents of India began the custom of placing symbolic marks on their foreheads. Although the exact reasons and time forehead marks

A Hindu holy woman marks her forehead with an intricate red design. *Reproduced by permission of AP/Wide World Photos.*

began has yet to be determined, some think the red markings had their roots in an ancient practice of blood sacrifice, that is, killing animals or people as an offering to the gods. Perhaps red marks were placed on the body as a symbol of the blood offering. Other experts have uncovered ancient religious rituals where worshippers wore garlands of leaves and cut symbols and shapes out of leaves to place on their foreheads.

The modern forehead markings worn by Indian people and those of Indian descent have different names, depending on the type of marking and what the marking is made of. Red dots are called bindi or pottu. They are usually made of a paste called kumkum, which is made of turmeric powder, a yellow spice, which is common in India. The yellow turmeric is mixed with lime juice, which turns it bright red. White lines are called tilak, which is the name of the sacred white ash that is used to make them. In addition to the forehead, tilak are often placed on the chin, neck, palms, and other parts of the body.

There are two basic types of forehead markings. Religious tilak and bindi are worn by both Hindu women and men and indicate which sect, or branch, of Hinduism the wearer belongs to. There are four major sects of the Hindu religion, depending on which gods are worshipped most devoutly, and each sect is recognized by different types of forehead markings. For example, those of the Vaishnav sect honor Lords Vishnu and Krishna and mark their heads with white lines in the shape of a "v." Followers of Lord Shiva are in the Saiv sect and mark their foreheads with three horizontal lines. Many Hindus believe that people have a "third eye," which sees spiritual truths, and that this third eye is located on the forehead above and between the eyes. Many Hindu temples keep kumkum paste at the entrance, and all who visit place a dot of it on their foreheads.

The second type of forehead marking is the bindi, or dot, worn over the third eye by many Indian women, which shows whether they are married. Young, unmarried women wear a black bindi, and married women wear a bright red bindi. Widows, whose husbands have died, either wear no bindi, or wear a white dot made of ash. Mothers sometimes place black bindi on the foreheads of babies and small children for protection against evil spirits. During the late twentieth century the bindi became a fashionable form of decoration, and rather than using the traditional powder women could buy red felt bindi that stuck on the forehead. Women began to use bindi of different decorative shapes and even use gemstones, like rhinestones and pearls, for a glamorous look.

FOR MORE INFORMATION

Gunda, Kavita, and Sangita Baruah. *What Is That?* Ann Arbor, MI: Proctor Publications, 1999.

Henna Stains

A reddish powder or paste made from the dried leaves of the henna bush, known by the scientific name of *Lawsonia inermis,* henna has been used to decorate the human body for thousands of years. Many historians believe that henna could have been used by people to decorate their hands and feet as long ago as 7000 B.C.E. After the religion of Islam, also known as the Muslim religion, was founded around 620 C.E., intricately patterned henna tattoos, also called mehndi, became an important part of Muslim culture in south Asia, Northern Africa, and the Middle East. Though there is evidence that some men have used henna decorations in the past, most henna decoration is done on the bodies of women and is created by female henna artists.

Mehndi is an ancient folk art in which tiny brushes and pens are used to apply a paste made of henna powder in patterns and shapes on various parts of the body, especially the hands and feet. After several hours the dried paste is removed, leaving a dark or reddish stain behind in the shape of the design. Muslim women have gathered for centuries for festive henna parties, where a henna artist, called a mu'allima, paints henna decorations on the guests. This has long been an important traditional preparation for a wedding, where the bride is painted with large and complex mehndi patterns, and

An Indian woman applying henna to the hand of a customer.
Reproduced by permission of © Jeffrey L. Rotman/ CORBIS.

the women of the wedding party receive smaller designs.

Like many body decorations, the use of henna may once have had a practical purpose. Some scholars think that ancient people of India, Africa, and the Middle East may have painted henna paste on the palms of their hands and soles of their feet to combat the fierce heat of their homelands. As the mehndi evolved from a solid covering into intricate designs, the patterns of the henna drawings began to have a purpose. Certain symbols and designs were supposed to ward off evil spirits, attract luck, or increase a bride's fertility.

During the 1980s and 1990s many rebellious American youth in the United States were unhappy with the isolation they felt in modern society. These youth began to seek and wear ancient tribal symbols in an effort to find or create a modern "tribe" to which they could belong. Some began to wear mehndi, spreading the use of henna stains beyond the Islamic, or Muslim, community into popular Western youth culture.

FOR MORE INFORMATION

All the Rage. Alexandria, VA: Time-Life Books, 1992.

Combs-Schilling, M. E. *Sacred Performances: Islam, Sexuality, and Sacrifice.* New York: Columbia University Press, 1990.

Kapchan, Deborah. *Gender on the Market: Moroccan Women and the Revoicing of Tradition.* Philadelphia, PA: University of Pennsylvania Press, 1996.

Jewelry

Jewelry has occupied an important part of life in India from ancient times to the present day. Evidence from the earliest Indus

Valley civilizations, which flourished along the Indus River in modern-day Pakistan and which date back to 2500 B.C.E., indicates that early Indians adorned themselves from head to toe with many varied ornaments. Although traditions have changed over the thousands of years since the beginning of Indian culture, jewelry remains an integral part of religious, regional, and social life.

Amulets

The earliest forms of jewelry were amulets, or ornaments worn to protect or empower the wearer. Ornaments worn by men symbolized their power over adversaries. Some ornaments, such as a specific headdress, could be worn only by certain members of a social group: those who inherited the right or earned it. The earliest forms of jewelry were made with flowers, especially orchids, which were inserted as ornaments in a hole in the earlobe of men and boys. Metal, ivory, or crystal ornaments also adorned the earlobes. Human hair taken from the decapitated head of an enemy was also a prized ornament for men. It symbolized a boy's rise to the status of warrior. The hair was often dyed red to symbolize the blood spurting from its victim. Tiger claws and those of the Indian anteater along with animal horns were also used to adorn the body. The Naga people of northeastern India continue to practice the ancient customs that archeologists, or scientists who study past cultures, believe ancient Indians began many thousands of years ago.

As societies grew and developed throughout India, jewelry styles became more elaborate. Jewelry continued to be worn as amulets, but the materials used became quite complex. Stones were polished into beads that were worn around the neck. Strings of red coral beads began to be worn by women and children to protect them from evil. Beads of amber, a fossilized clear or yellowish substance from a cone-bearing tree, were worn to protect the health of the wearer. Traditional Indian medical practices suggest that amber will protect against sore throats and that yellow amber prevents jaundice, a deficiency of vitamin D that causes the skin to turn yellow. More elaborate amulets began to be made of metal and jewels. These amulets took many forms, including intricately engraved plates with symbols of gods and weapon-shaped amulets in the form of arrowheads and knives.

Jewelry from head to toe

The Mogul Empire, Indian Muslims who ruled India from 1500 to 1700 C.E., greatly influenced Indian jewelry styles. Under Mogul rule Indian goldsmiths developed the technical skill to create beautiful jewels for the body, and Indians wore an almost infinite variety of jewelry that literally covered the wearer from head to toe.

A woman adorned in traditional Indian jewelry, including bracelets, earrings, and necklaces.
Reproduced by permission of © Charles & Josette Lenars/ CORBIS.

Indian men typically wore less jewelry than women, but the varieties available to men were plentiful. Upon their heads men could adorn their turbans with pearl-tipped heron bird feathers, a fan of jewels, or an ornament shaped like a bird with a strand of pearls in its beak. Around their necks, men hung pendants, strands of pearls, or amulets made of precious metal inlaid with gemstones. Hinged armbands and bracelets adorned their upper arms and wrists.

Indians wore many rings on their fingers. Especially prized were signet rings, small circular rings with unique marks on them which were worn on the little finger or the middle finger of the right hand, and archer's thumb rings. Worn by Hindus since ancient times, signet rings were considered good luck amulets by Buddhists from the first to the tenth centuries, and prized by Muslims from the twelfth century. The archer's thumb ring was used to increase the accuracy and distance of an arrow and became popular in India during the Mogul Empire. A curved ring made of stone, especially jade, the archer's ring is worn with the curved tip pointing toward the wrist between the thumb and the forefinger. Wealthier men wore archer's rings made of gold and inlaid with gems, including diamonds and rubies.

The lower part of the body was also ornamented. A baldric, or a special belt worn diagonally across the chest from the left shoulder, supported a sword but was also a beautiful ornament made of gold brocade with enameled pieces and gemstones. Men's ankles were circled with chain bracelets. Although only the wealthiest Indian men wore this type of jewelry, they represent the extent of jewelry styles that were popular during the Mogul Empire. These styles continue to be worn in India, especially in rural areas of the north.

Women's jewelry

Women wore more jewelry than men. During the Mogul Empire women adorned their heads with coins, chains worn over their foreheads, strands of pearls, and ornaments made to look like flowers. They also had hair ornaments made of gold and jewels that covered the long braids that reached their waist. Multiple piercings in their noses as well as their ears allowed for more jewelry to be worn. Bracelets and armbands were worn in groups. Some women covered their entire upper and lower arm in bangles, wearing fifty or more at a time to signify their marriage. For ceremonies, each finger was covered with a ring attached to a chain that covered the back of the wearer's hand and attached to a bracelet with more chains. Women's waists were circled with gold belts, some with bells strung on them. Women's feet were adorned with elaborate jewelry, including toe rings and anklets.

Women wore jewelry daily, but wedding ceremonies required the most decoration. Jewelry signifying a woman's married status is very important in Indian culture. Rather than using a wedding ring as Western cultures do, Indians use a variety of regional types of ornament. In northern India women wear specific ornaments on the head, nose, wrist, and toes, while in southern India ornaments called thali signify marriage. Many other regional variations also exist. Some wear silver anklets and toe rings. Women often wear special jewelry during their wedding ceremonies and some continue to wear this jewelry during the first year of their marriage for luck.

Many traditional Indian jewelry styles continue to be worn by modern Indian women, but those living in cities have adopted Western styles as well.

FOR MORE INFORMATION

Untracht, Oppi. *Traditional Jewelry of India.* New York: Harry N. Abrams, 1997.

Piercing

The abundance of jewelry in Indian culture has required the use of piercing to secure some important ornaments. The ears of women and sometimes men and the noses of men are the most common areas for piercing. Practiced since ancient times, piercing continues to be an important part of Indian culture.

In India the ears are often pierced in multiple places and elaborate earrings are hung from the holes. The placement of the piercing is determined by religious, regional, or ethnic customs. In some areas in southern India, for example, the ear lobes of female infants used to be pierced and stretched so that by the time she reached thirteen years old, the girl's earlobes hung almost to her shoulders. This practice signified wealth and virtue among women from ancient times, and females without stretched lobes were shunned or considered prostitutes. This particular custom began to disappear in the nineteenth century as Christian missionaries converted people in these areas.

Piercing the nose has special significance in Indian culture. In rural areas female infants' noses are pierced to protect them from evil spirits and illness. Nose ornaments have been used in India since at least 1250 C.E., when Muslims were invading the area from central Asia and Persia (present-day Iran), where use of nose ornaments was customary. The nose ring has since become very important in Indian culture as a symbol of a woman's marital status. Women wear a nose ring only while their husband is living. Nose ornaments include studs pierced through the side of the nose, rings threaded through the septum (or central part of the nose), and large hoops adorned with jewels hooked through one nostril and supported by a chain secured in the hair or to headwear.

A woman displays her traditional Indian nose piercings. The placement of piercings are often determined by religious, regional, or ethnic customs. *Reproduced by permission of © Sheldan Collins/ CORBIS.*

FOR MORE INFORMATION

Untracht, Oppi. *Traditional Jewelry of India.* New York: Harry N. Abrams, 1997.

Indian Footwear

In the chilly Himalayan mountain northern regions of India, a variety of boots and shoes have been made over the centuries to protect the feet from cold and rainy weather. These boots and shoes are made of leather, wool, and plant fibers. But since the weather in most of India is warm, shoes were not necessary, and for much of history, Indians went barefoot. Without the need for footwear, Indian culture developed a unique history of praising the feet. Mothers massage the feet of their babies. Youth honor the feet of elders. Someone seeks forgiveness at the feet of his or her victim. Lovers caress each other's feet to show their devotion. Indians traditionally keep their feet as clean as their hands, and even today villages often have at least one craftsman devoted to the manufacture of products to clean the feet, especially foot scrubbers made of stone or metal. Literature written as early as 2500 B.C.E. documents the use of toe rings, ankle bracelets, and foot ornaments. Indian religious and romantic literature abounds with references to the power of the feet, indicating their cultural significance.

But in the areas of India where shoes are not necessary because of the warm weather, footwear, although not worn daily, has become an important part of religious devotion and other ceremonies. Ceremonial footwear is beautifully made, decorated with embroidery, inlaid with precious stones and metals, and adorned with bells and tassels. Feet are also painted, dyed, and covered in ornament for special occasions. Footwear used for ceremony varies from region to region due to India's many different ethnic and cultural groups. Some of the most common types of shoes worn in India are toe-knob sandals called padukas, strapped sandals referred to as chappals, pointed shoes known as juttis, and tall boots called khapusa.

FOR MORE INFORMATION

Jain-Neubauer, Jutta. *Feet and Footwear in Indian Culture.* Toronto, Canada: Bata Shoe Museum, 2000.

Chappals

Chappals, a simple type of leather sandal, provide the foot with basic protection from hot surfaces and rough terrain. Made with flat soles attached to the foot by straps that encircle the top of the foot and big toe, chappals became a common type of footwear in India by the third century C.E. and remain the most typical foot covering today. Chappals are popular among men, women, and children of all religions throughout India and surrounding countries such as Pakistan, Bangladesh, and Sri Lanka.

In the early twentieth century the great Indian leader Mahatma Gandhi (1869–1948) inspired Indians to make their own chappals in addition to weaving their own cloth as a symbol of Indian independence at a time when Indians were trying to end British rule of their land. His efforts worked, and small family-run shoe businesses succeeded in India. During the 1970s, when handmade Indian chappals became popular in the United States and Europe with hippies, young people who rejected mass-produced clothing among other conventions of Western society, these small Indian shops were able to export most or all of their chappals for profit.

Chappals are only one type of sandal found in India. Each region throughout India, especially the northern regions, produces a variety of sandal styles. Some are embellished with embroidery, and others have wooden soles decorated with carvings. The variations are almost infinite.

FOR MORE INFORMATION

Jain-Neubauer, Jutta. *Feet and Footwear in Indian Culture.* Toronto, Canada: Bata Shoe Museum, 2000.

Jutti

The jutti is a shoe worn by men, women, and children throughout India. Most often made of leather from the hide of buffalo, camels, or cows, juttis can also have uppers, or the tops of the shoe, formed from other textiles. Juttis are heavily decorated with cotton, silk, or golden embroidery and sometimes wool pompons, or tufts of material. The jutti is identified by its pointed toe and flat, straight sole that does not distinguish between left or right foot. The shoe can have a closed or open heel, and there are many regional variations in toe style and decoration. Some regional styles are specially named. For example, Salim Shahi juttis, which have a curled toe point and a decoratively curved upper, are named after a Mogul prince of the 1600s.

The jutti evolved from a shoe style with a curled up pointed toe called mojari, worn by the wealthiest male citizens during the Mogul Empire in the early sixteenth century. From the tips of mojari, pendants, bells, and beads are often suspended. Mojari continue to be worn for weddings and other special occasions in India.

FOR MORE INFORMATION

Jain-Neubauer, Jutta. *Feet and Footwear in Indian Culture.* Toronto, Canada: Bata Shoe Museum, 2000.

Khapusa

Khapusas were heavy boots that covered the knees. Made to protect the wearer from snow, snakes, stones, and the cold, khapusas were worn in northern India, especially in the Himalayan Mountains, from the first century C.E.

Boots are thought to have been brought to India by foreigners. Boots were a common foot covering of early invaders from central Asia, including the Moguls, Afghans, and Persians. The ancient Indian rulers of the Kushan Empire, which flourished in what is now Pakistan, Afghanistan, and northwest India from about 50 to the mid-second century C.E. were among the first to bring khapusas to India. Many depictions and statues of foreigners in India show them wearing heavy boots. No early examples of khapusas remain, but recovered paintings and sculptural artifacts suggest that the boots were made of heavy leather, sometimes decorated with patterns.

Boots were practical for those living in the cold mountains of northern India, but most Indians went barefoot when weather permitted. Other than mountain dwellers, the only other people to regularly wear boots were horsemen and soldiers.

FOR MORE INFORMATION

Jain-Neubauer, Jutta. *Feet and Footwear in Indian Culture.* Toronto, Canada: Bata Shoe Museum, 2000.

Paduka

The paduka—also known as the khadaun, kharawan, and karom—is the simplest type of Indian foot protection. At its most basic, a paduka is a wooden sole with a knob that fits between the big toe and the second toe. The wearer grips the knob between his toes to keep the sole on the foot. First worn by mendicants, or religious men, padukas have been part of Indian costume since at least the seventh century C.E. In modern times padukas are rarely worn, yet they are still valued as symbols of religious devotion. They are often given as gifts or worn at religious ceremonies.

Padukas fit well with the simple life of religious men, who often lived with the fewest necessities as a way of practicing spiritual discipline. Padukas provided protection for the feet in the simplest manner. Made of durable materials, padukas saved the feet from the heat of summer roads and the pain of sharp stones and thorns. One pair of padukas discovered in the eighteenth century adds another dimension to the sandal's ritual use, however. This pair of padukas was made of wood with a bed of sharp iron spikes covering the footbed. The wearer must have suffered pain with every step as a way of reinforcing his religious convictions.

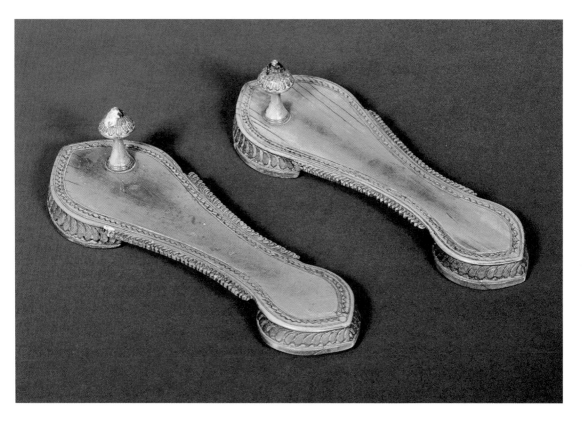

Although all padukas are soles with a toe knob, not all padukas are simple. Some are lavishly decorated and made of expensive materials such as ivory, leather, silver, or rare wood. While common padukas are cut in the shape of a footprint, padukas for celebratory or ritual occasions are cut in the shape of fish, hourglasses, or feet with carved toes. These special occasion padukas are made with great care. Expertly carved, painted, or inlaid with silver and gold, they are quite luxurious. One pair of intricately painted wooden padukas featured toe knobs topped with ivory lotus flowers that turned from bud to blossom as each step triggered a mechanism in the sole.

The paduka has a wooden sole and a knob that fits between the big toe and the second toe. *Reproduced by permission of © Angelo Hornak/CORBIS.*

FOR MORE INFORMATION

Jain-Neubauer, Jutta. *Feet and Footwear in Indian Culture.* Toronto, Canada: Bata Shoe Museum, 2000.

Life in Ancient Greece

Life in ancient Greece developed from three significant civilizations: the Minoans, the Mycenaeans, and the ancient Greeks. Archeologists, scientists who study the remains of ancient cultures, have studied these civilizations and have found evidence of sophisticated societies. In all three of these civilizations the evidence indicates that ancient Greeks used clothing for much more than simply protecting the body from the elements. Clothing for these civilizations served as decoration and signaled the status of the wearer. The wealthiest citizens adorned themselves in fine fabrics and wore elaborate jewelry that required great skill to create, while the poorest dressed in basic, coarsely made garments.

The first Greeks: Minoans and Mycenaeans

Minoans are considered the first Greeks. Minoan civilization developed on the Greek island of Crete around 3000 B.C.E. Their society was ruled from several large palaces and involved complex systems of trade with others, including the Egyptians. Minoan civilization survived for several hundred years, but archeologists are uncertain why this society failed. Some guess that Minoans suffered natural disasters, such as volcanic explosions on the nearby island of Thera that caused tidal waves or earthquakes on Crete.

Evidence of Minoan life comes from excavated, or dug out, palace sites in Crete where archeologists have discovered pottery, statues, and frescoes, a form of paint applied directly to a wall's wet plaster. These artifacts tell a story of Minoan life and show what people wore while performing everything from the everyday tasks of fishing and trading to participating in religious ceremonies.

Not long after the Minoan culture disappeared in about 1600 B.C.E., the Mycenaean culture began to flourish on mainland Greece and invaded Crete. Mycenaeans developed small kingdoms that traded with each other and spoke the same language but did not unite under a centralized ruler. Each kingdom was ruled from an acropolis, a set of important buildings, such as the royal palace and soldiers' houses, located on the highest ground of the city. Each kingdom had a main city that was protected by an encircling wall, but most of the people lived outside the city wall. The discovery of bronze armor indicates that the Mycenaeans were warlike and that small kingdoms often fought with each other. In addition, although Mycenaeans brought their own language and culture to Greece, frescoes and pottery show depictions of Mycenaean clothing that clearly shows the influence of Minoan culture. The greatest source of information about the Mycenaeans has been found in royal tombs, which include objects that offer insight into their daily lives and religious beliefs. Although both the Minoans and Mycenaeans developed a system of writing, only information recording the trade of livestock and farm produce and the tasks of palace officials have been found.

Early Greek society

A series of famines and other environmental catastrophes around 1200 B.C.E. caused the Mycenaean culture to erode, and Mycenaeans dispersed to other areas. There is no exact information about where the Mycenaeans moved to, but some archeologists believe that they became the ancestors of the Etruscans who later came to power in what is now Italy, just before the rise of Roman society. As the Mycenaeans left Greece, another culture began to flourish. The Dorians, ancient Greeks, became dominant and conquered the struggling Mycenaeans, some who remained and settled in southern Greece. As the Dorians took power, Greek culture plunged into a period called the Dark Ages, which lasted from about 1100 to 800 B.C.E. During this time, not much is known about life in

Greece because no artwork, writing, or metalwork from the period has been discovered.

By about 800 B.C.E. Greek culture began to flourish again with increasing population, the development of trade colonies, and the rediscovery of the skill of writing. As Greek colonies developed into independent states, which all shared the same language, culture, and religion, Greece entered what is known as the Archaic Period (800–480 B.C.E.). Within the Greek states people were divided between free men, which included the wives and children of these landowning citizens, and slaves. Greek states were governed by free men in a system of government called an oligarchy, or rule by the few, for some years but during the later years of this period tyrants, or single powerful men, took control of whole cities. Evidence about life in Greece during the Archaic Period comes mainly from the states of Athens and Sparta in the central part of Greece.

The period from 500 to 336 B.C.E. is considered the Classical Period of Greek history. During this time Athens dominated Greek

The ancient Greek temple of Juno, one of many temples built to honor the Greek gods. All aspects of Greek living were influenced by their beliefs in gods and mythology. *Reproduced by permission of AP/Wide World Photos.*

business, culture, and politics. The ideas about art, architecture, philosophy, politics, and literature that developed during this period laid the foundation of modern Western civilization. One of the biggest changes to Greek life in Athens was the emergence of democracy, or rule by the people. Citizens of Greek cities overthrew their tyrants and set up governments ruled by citizens. Although citizens could speak and vote in this early form of democracy, women, slaves, and those born outside the city were excluded. At the same time Sparta became the most powerful military force in Greece and emphasized the health and vigor of its population. Developing strong soldiers was that state's primary focus. Women were encouraged to keep fit so that they would give birth to healthy babies, and only newborns with no sign of defect or weakness were allowed to live. As Athenian and Spartan societies became more and more focused on different priorities, conflict between the states arose that ended in a war that Sparta won in 404 B.C.E. This war started a series of smaller wars that resulted in Philip II (383–336 B.C.E.) of Macedonia, an area in the northeast of Greece, coming to power in 359 B.C.E. Philip's son Alexander (356–323 B.C.E.) became king of Macedonia in 336 B.C.E. He soon earned the title Alexander the Great and ruled the largest empire in the world, encompassing Greece and vast areas of modern-day Egypt, Spain, and India. Upon Alexander's death in 323 B.C.E. his empire became unstable as various people tried to seize control of different areas. Wars broke out throughout the empire over the next one hundred years. The end of Greek dominance in the region occurred in 146 B.C.E. when Romans began ruling the area.

As the political life in Greece changed over the years and the geographic boundaries shifted, Greek culture developed sophisticated ideas about clothing and appearance. Craftsmen fine-tuned their skills in weaving cloth, tanning leather, making jewelry, and decorating garments with paint and embroidery. These advancements occurred alongside advancements in other parts of Greek life, including the arts, architecture, philosophy, law, and military strategy. Though the ancient Greeks' ideas about life continue to influence modern cultures, clothing styles have changed a great deal.

FOR MORE INFORMATION

Chisholm, Jane, Lisa Miles, and Struan Reid. *The Usborne Encyclopedia of Ancient Greece.* London, England: Usborne Publishing, 1999.

Houston, Mary G. *Ancient Greek, Roman, and Byzantine Costume and Decoration.* 2nd ed. New York: Barnes and Noble, 1947.

Payne, Blanche, Geitel Winakor, and Jane Farrell-Beck. *The History of Costume: From Ancient Mesopotamia Through the Twentieth Century.* 2nd ed. New York: HarperCollins, 1992.

Symons, David J. *Costume of Ancient Greece.* New York: Chelsea House, 1987.

Greek Clothing

The history of clothing in ancient Greece traces its roots to three significant civilizations: the Minoans, the Mycenaeans, and the ancient Greeks. Each of these civilizations created sophisticated clothing customs. Clothing for these civilizations served not only to cover and protect the body, but also to decorate and enhance the beauty of the wearer.

Minoan clothing

The Minoan culture developed on the Greek island of Crete in about 3000 B.C.E. Minoans created a thriving society around royal palaces and survived for several hundred years. Archeologists, scientists who study the remains of ancient cultures, have excavated sites in Crete to find pottery, frescoes (paintings applied directly to wet plaster on walls) on the walls of palace remains, and statues. These artifacts provide a vivid picture of Minoan culture, especially that of the wealthy citizens.

Minoan remains indicate that Minoan clothing fit the contours of the body and required knowledge of sewing techniques. Men wore a variety of loin coverings and rarely covered their upper bodies. Women wore tiered, bell-shaped skirts and fitted short-sleeved tops that exposed the breasts. Minoans seemed to idealize tiny waists, and both men and women wore tightly fitted belts, or girdles, that cinched their waists down to a fashionably small size.

Mycenaean clothing

When the Minoan culture disappeared in about 1600 B.C.E., for reasons archeologists still have yet to discover, the Mycenaean culture began to flourish on mainland Greece and invaded Crete,

Greek clothing usually consisted of long, flowing garments, head wreaths, and sandals. *Reproduced by permission of © Archivo Iconografico, S.A./CORBIS.*

where they encountered the Minoans. The remains of Minoan culture influenced the Mycenaeans who adopted many of their clothing styles. Women's clothing is especially difficult to distinguish from Minoan clothing. Women wore the same long skirts and short-sleeved tops; however, paintings indicate that Mycenaean women did occasionally cover their breasts with a bib or blouse. Mycenaean men appear to have worn loin coverings similar to the Minoans, but more frequently they seem to have worn short-sleeved tunics with a belted waist. The true distinguishing costumes of the Mycenaeans were their armor. Evidence indicates that Mycenaeans were warlike peoples. For battle Mycenaean soldiers wore protective clothing that wrapped the body from neck to thigh in bronze plates, bronze leg guards, and helmets constructed of boar's tusks.

Greek clothing

As the Mycenaean culture began to suffer from famines and other environmental catastrophes around 1200 B.C.E., another culture began to flourish. The Dorians, ancient Greeks, became dominant and conquered the struggling Mycenaeans. Although no evidence about what Greeks wore has been discovered for life between the twelfth and the eighth centuries B.C.E., by the eighth century art was again being produced and paintings of Greek clothing styles appeared. As one can see in many examples from Greek art, the ancient Greeks had a great appreciation for the beauty of the naked body. Early Greek society did not forbid public nakedness, at least for men. Men always went naked when exercising or competing in athletic games, and both men and women bathed naked in public baths, though not together. Women were required to keep their bodies covered when they were with men.

By the seventh century B.C.E. Greek society was dominated by a wealthy class who wore luxurious woven clothes and decorative jewelry. From this time until the invasion of and defeat by the Romans in 146 B.C.E., Greeks developed several different styles of clothes. In general, Greeks did not cut and sew their clothes until the fourth century B.C.E. Instead they draped finely woven cloth over and around their bodies to create distinct styles of dress and protective wraps. The wealthiest Greeks could afford fine wool and finely woven linen, which at its most expensive was an almost transparent, soft cloth. Others used cloth woven from the flax plant soaked in olive oil, and peasants used textiles made of coarse wool. The most distinctive Greek garment is the chiton, or tunic. Two different styles of chiton were developed: the Ionic chiton and the Doric chiton, with variations, usually of length, to distinguish styles for men and women. The fabric of chitons was crinkled, or pleated, to enhance the fullness of the drape of the garment. Over the chiton, Greeks kept themselves warm with a variety of wraps, including the himation, chlamys, chlaina, and diplax. Although these draped fashions continued to be popular, by the fourth century B.C.E. both women and men began wearing sewn tunics with a U or V neckline. Writings from this time discuss a variety of specific styles for these sewn tunics and archeologists uncovered a variety of tunic styles in a temple in Attica, a state of Greece that formed the territory of Athens, the Greek cultural center.

Because much of our knowledge of Greek fashions comes from the marble sculptures they left behind, many people once thought that most Greeks wore only white clothes. However, experts now know that even the pale marble of the statues was once covered with bright paint that wore off over the centuries. Greeks, in fact, loved color and many dyed their clothes. Wealthy aristocrats wore purple clothes dyed from a species of shellfish or pure white linen robes. Yellow clothes were worn mostly by women. Black clothes were worn by those mourning the death of a loved one. Peasants dyed their clothing a variety of greens, browns, and grays. Soldiers wore dark red garments to minimize the appearance of blood on the battlefield.

In addition to dyeing, decorative designs were also painted, embroidered, or woven onto garments in many colors. Garments were also adorned with patterns of geometric shapes or trimmed with colorful border designs.

FOR MORE INFORMATION

Batterberry, Michael, and Ariane Batterberry. *Fashion: The Mirror of History.* New York: Greenwich House, 1982.

Norris, Herbert. *Costume and Fashion: The Evolution of European Dress Through the Earlier Ages.* London, England: J. M. Dent and Sons, 1924. Reprint, New York: E. P. Dutton, 1931.

Payne, Blanche, Geitel Winakor, and Jane Farrell-Beck. *The History of Costume: From Ancient Mesopotamia Through the Twentieth Century.* 2nd ed. New York: HarperCollins, 1992.

Symons, David J. *Costume of Ancient Greece.* New York: Chelsea House, 1987.

Chlaina and Diplax

During the Classical Period of Greece (500–336 B.C.E.) typical clothing was largely made up of woven rectangles of fabric, usually wool or linen, which were draped in different ways about the body. It was how a piece of cloth was used, rather than the design of the piece itself, which gave it its name. Though most forms of classical Greek clothing were worn by both men and women, there were a few items that were intended to be used mainly by one sex or the other. The chlaina and the diplax were two forms of outer clothing primarily worn by women. They were both types of cloaks, which were wrapped around the body for warmth and protection. The chlaina was usually worn by women at work, who draped the long fabric as a protective overskirt around their hips, often over the chiton, or tunic, they wore. The diplax, which gets its name from the Greek word for "double," was usually larger than the chlaina and was wrapped around the shoulders over the chiton for warmth and modesty. Another name sometimes given to the diplax was "cholene."

Like many Greek clothes, the chlaina and diplax were sometimes designed with decorative geometric patterns around the borders or dyed in bright colors. Metal weights were also often sewn into the corners of these garments to help the wearer drape them more beautifully.

FOR MORE INFORMATION

Pistolese, Rosana, and Ruth Horsting. *History of Fashions.* New York: John Wiley and Sons, 1970.

Symons, David. *Costume of Ancient Greece.* Broomall, PA: Chelsea House Publishers, 1988.

Chlamys

Chlamys, like the one worn by the man on the left, offered warmth and decoration and were often adorned with clavi, or purple stripes. *Reproduced by permission of © Bettmann/CORBIS.*

The most common cloak worn by young Greek men between the seventh and first centuries B.C.E., the chlamys (KLA-mis) was one of the few items of ancient Greek clothing worn exclusively by men. It was a short cape, fashioned, like most Greek styles, from a single rectangle of fabric fastened with a pin at one shoulder. Woven of coarse woolen cloth, the chlamys offered the wearer warmth and protection from the weather, while still giving freedom of movement to the active Greek man.

Until the later part of the fourth century B.C.E., when Macedonian general Alexander the Great's (356–323 B.C.E.) conquests of Persia and Egypt brought new fashion influences to Greece, most Greek garments had for centuries been worn by both men and women. Men and women might wear their chitons (tunics) and himations (cloaks) draped differently, or have them decorated with different colors and designs, but few garments were designed to be worn by one sex alone. The chlamys was one piece of clothing that was worn only by men. It was a short, warm cloak that was preferred by soldiers, horsemen, and travelers, and those who wanted to imitate the dashing fashions of these adventurous young men.

Usually a rectangle of woven wool, measuring approximately seventy-two inches by fifty-four inches, the chlamys could also be rounded at the edges. The cloak was worn by draping it over the left shoulder and pinning it together over the right shoulder. This left the right arm free to hold a sword or a horse's reins, while covering most of the rest of the upper body. Popular with travelers, the chlamys could also be used as a blanket when camping overnight. Often, metal weights were sewn into the corners of the fabric, to help the wearer drape his cape in an elegant fashion.

Though many Greek men wore the chlamys over some other garment, such as a chiton, it was just as common to wear the cloak alone. In many works of Greek art, messengers, who carried communications between the Greek cities and towns, are shown wearing only the chlamys and a wide brimmed traveling hat called a petasos, both of which were typical traveling clothes of the time.

FOR MORE INFORMATION

Bigelow, Marybelle S. *Fashion in History: Western Dress, Prehistoric to Present.* Minneapolis, MN: Burgess Publishing, 1970.

Laver, James. *Costume and Fashion: A Concise History.* New York: Thames and Hudson, 2002.

Doric Chiton

The Doric chiton (KYE-ten) was one of the most common garments worn by both men and women in Greece during the sixth and early fifth centuries B.C.E. The Dorians were a people who had invaded Greece in the twelfth century B.C.E., and the Doric style was a simple, classic design found in much Greek art and fashion. The chiton was a kind of tunic formed by folding and wrapping a single rectangular piece of fabric around the body. Women's chitons usually provided more modesty, reaching from shoulders to ankle, while men often wore their chitons at knee length. However, for formal or ceremonial occasions, men sometimes wore the long chiton as well.

Most Greek clothing was created simply and elegantly, by draping and wrapping a single piece of cloth in different ways. The earliest form of the chiton was simply a rectangle of woven wool cloth, approximately twice the width of the wearer, which was folded around the body in a narrow tube and fastened at the shoulders with pins or broaches. The Doric chiton, also sometimes called the Doric peplos, appeared around 500 B.C.E. and was made from a much larger piece of woolen fabric, which allowed it to be pleated and draped. The rectangular chiton was folded down at the top before being wrapped around the wearer, creating a short cape or overblouse at the top. This overblouse was called the apotygma, and it was sometimes weighted at the edges with beads or pieces of metal so that it would stay in place.

Once it was pinned at the shoulders, the chiton could be belted to increase the drapery effect. Both men and women draped the Doric chiton artistically, but men often wore it pinned at only one shoulder, leaving the other shoulder bare. Another common male style was to drape a belt or sash around the back of the neck, then under the arms to tie in back, creating a sort of harness to hold the chiton in place. Women frequently wore several belts or girdles with the Doric chiton. Sometimes as many as three belts were worn, one under the breasts, one at the waist, and one at the hips, to catch up the flowing fabric and drape it gracefully. Another feminine style involved wrapping one long belt around the body and crossing it between the breasts or across the back.

Because much of the information about Greek fashions has come from marble statues, many people have long assumed that ancient Greeks dressed mainly in white. However, historians have learned from documents and other studies that colored clothing was very popular among Greeks who could afford the dyes. Doric chitons were often dyed in colors and striped designs, and decorative borders were also popular.

Around the mid-400s B.C.E., the simple Doric chiton was replaced in popular fashion by the more elaborate Ionic chiton.

FOR MORE INFORMATION

Bigelow, Marybelle S. *Fashion in History: Western Dress, Prehistoric to Present.* Minneapolis, MN: Burgess Publishing, 1970.

Norris, Herbert. *Costume and Fashion: The Evolution of European Dress Through the Earlier Ages.* London, England: J. M. Dent and Sons, 1924. Reprint, New York: E. P. Dutton, 1931.

[*See also* **Volume 1, Ancient Greece: Ionic Chiton**]

▪ Himation

Both Greek men and women wore an outer garment called a himation (hi-MA-tee-on) beginning as early as the sixth century B.C.E. Although made in various dimensions, himations generally were large rectangular pieces of fabric arranged around the body in a variety of different ways. They were made out of loosely woven thick wool. Though no physical remnants of himations have been discovered, statues and decorations found on pottery suggest that these garments were often dyed bright colors and covered or bordered with intricate designs that were either woven into the fabric or painted on.

Men normally wore the himation alone, although some wore it over a short chiton, a basic garment that covered the upper body and varying portions of the legs, much like a short dress. When men wore himations, they made sure to keep the edges from dragging on the ground because to do so was considered in poor taste. Fashionable men carefully wrapped their himation over their left shoulder, because to bare one's left shoulder was a sign of barbarism, or being uncivilized. Himations were popular with men until the end of the Archaic Period, around 500 B.C.E., when the himation became most frequently worn by women.

Greek women wore himations in public as warm cloaks over their thin Ionic chitons (a type of tunic). Women wore himations in a variety of different styles, such as the symmetrical and the transverse himations. A symmetrical himation was a large rectangular piece of cloth worn draped over the shoulders like a shawl with the center sometimes pulled up to cover the head. A transverse himation became popular to wear over the Ionic chiton; it was made out of a rectangular cloth with the center touching the left hip of the wearer and the ends attached over the right shoulder with a brooch or pin. One of the most common ways for women to drape the himation was to wrap it around the entire body. Starting with an end of the cloth draped forward over the left shoulder, the himation would be wrapped across the back and either under the right arm or covering the right arm and then slung across the chest to the left shoulder or held over the left arm. To secure the himation, some Greek women tucked a fold into their girdle, a string wrapped around their waist. Less often women tied their himation around their hips. For greatest protection from the weather, women would completely cover themselves with their himations, draping the cloth over their heads to veil their faces and covering both their arms with it.

Himations were such a prevalent part of the Greek wardrobe for so many years and worn in so many different styles that the word "himation" is often used by scholars to refer to any number of different wraps worn by Greeks.

FOR MORE INFORMATION

Houston, Mary G. *Ancient Greek, Roman, and Byzantine Costume and Decoration.* 2nd ed. New York: Barnes and Noble, 1947.

Symons, David J. *Costume of Ancient Greece.* New York: Chelsea House, 1987.

[*See also* **Volume 1, Ancient Greece: Doric Chiton; Volume 1, Ancient Greece: Ionic Chiton**]

Over their clothing Greek women often draped a himation, which could vary in color from basic white to a more colorful pink or red. *Reproduced by permission of © Araldo de Luca/CORBIS.*

Ionic Chiton

Ionia is an eastern region of Greece, and Ionian design is a delicate, elegant style that became popular throughout Greece in art,

The woman on the right wears the traditional Doric chiton, which was less intricate than the Ionic chiton, worn by the woman on the left. *Reproduced by permission of © Bettmann/CORBIS.*

architecture, and fashion during the fifth century B.C.E. The Ionic chiton (KITE-en), the most popular Greek garment during the fifth century B.C.E., demonstrates many of the elaborate features of Ionian design. More of a gown than a tunic, the Ionic chiton was an intricately draped garment with many folds and pleats. It was worn by both men and women.

Like the Doric chiton and the peplos, a simple sleeveless outer garment, the Ionic chiton was formed from a single rectangular piece of fabric. However, while the earlier Dorian garments had been made of wool, the Ionic chiton was made from much lighter linen fabric, dyed in bright colors and embroidered with stars, birds, or other designs. Some Ionic chitons were even woven of silk. This lighter fabric allowed much more pleating than had been possible with wool, which created fuller, more flowing garments. Ionic chitons were also much larger than earlier chitons, often measuring twice the width of the wearer's outstretched arms. This allowed plenty of fabric to make the pleats and folds that were the most important feature of the Ionic design. Those who wore the Ionic chiton often increased the folds and drapery of the garment by tightly folding and twisting the fabric when wet, then allowing it to dry in order to set the folds in the cloth.

Unlike the Doric chiton or peplos, the Ionic chiton was not folded over at the top to create an overblouse. Instead, the fabric was wrapped around the wearer and pinned along the shoulders and arms in as many as eight to ten places. Once the chiton was belted below the breasts or at the waist, the pinned shoulders formed elbow-length sleeves that covered the arms with soft folds of fabric. The fabric was usually bloused out above the belt to form more folds. Both women and men sometimes wrapped a belt behind the neck and around the shoulders to hold the chiton in place during physical activity. Women almost always wore the Ionic chiton so long it reached the floor. Young men often wore a shorter, knee-length version, while older men and men of high office wore ankle-length chitons. Since the Ionic chiton was made of sheer, lightweight fabric, a woolen peplos or Doric chiton was sometimes layered over it for protection from the cold or a himation, or cloak, was wrapped around the wearer.

Greek styles have inspired fashion designers through the ages, and the graceful Ionic chiton is one of the most typical examples of the elegance of Greek clothing. In 1907 Spanish designer Mariano Fortuny (1871–1949) created a popular dress called the Delphos gown, which was based on the design of the Ionic chiton.

FOR MORE INFORMATION

Bigelow, Marybelle S. *Fashion in History: Western Dress, Prehistoric to Present.* Minneapolis, MN: Burgess Publishing, 1970.

Hope, Thomas. *Costumes of the Greeks and Romans.* New York: Dover, 1962.

Norris, Herbert. *Costume and Fashion: The Evolution of European Dress through the Earlier Ages.* London, England: J. M. Dent and Sons, 1924. Reprint, New York: E. P. Dutton, 1931.

[*See also* **Volume 1, Ancient Greece: Doric Chiton; Volume 1, Ancient Greece: Himation**]

Loin Coverings

Mycenaean men living on the mainland of what would become Greece in about 1600 B.C.E. and Minoan men living on the Greek island of Crete around 3000 B.C.E. wore several basic styles of loin coverings and usually left their upper bodies bare. These styles developed over time and were adapted as clothes for laborers or undergarments in later Greek society.

Worn by Mycenaeans and Minoans, the kilt, or schenti, was a thigh-length skirt with a tasseled point in front that hung between the knees. The kilt was held around the waist by a tight belt. Kilts were often made with elaborate designs and are believed to be the costume of only the wealthiest men. Pictures of these Mycenaean and Minoan kilts remain on frescoes, paintings done directly on plaster walls, and pottery from the period. Similar schenti had also been worn by wealthy Egyptians as early as 2700 B.C.E.

Loin skirts called aprons were worn by men of all classes. Men wore either a single or a double apron. A single apron was a rectangle of cloth that covered the man's buttocks and hung to mid thigh. Single aprons were worn with a codpiece, a covering for the man's genitals. A double apron covered both the front and the back of a man from waist to mid thigh. The front of a double apron was

Various Minoans on the Greek island of Crete wearing the loin coverings that helped protect them from the elements. *Reproduced by permission of © CORBIS.*

slightly shorter than the back. Both styles of aprons were worn with belts.

Although upper-class men in later Greek society would more often drape cloths over their upper bodies, these early Minoan and Mycenaean costumes survived into later ancient Greek society as what became known as the zoma, or loincloth, a piece of cloth wrapped around the waist like a short skirt. Male and female athletes wore zoma for competitions, warriors wore it under armor, both men and women used zoma as undergarments, and slaves and other laborers wore it alone as a practical garment for work.

FOR MORE INFORMATION

Symons, David J. *Costume of Ancient Greece.* New York: Chelsea House, 1987.

[*See also* Volume 1, Ancient Egypt: Schenti]

Military Dress

Warriors in ancient Greece developed many methods of protecting themselves in battle. Mycenaeans, who ruled Greece as early as 1600 B.C.E., crafted armor out of bronze plates. Soldiers wore suits made of bronze plates held together with leather straps. This armor protected the body from the neck to the upper thighs. Soldiers strapped additional bronze plates over their shins for leg protection and wore helmets made of boar's tusks. Mycenaean soldiers also carried a variety of different wooden framed shields and bronze daggers and swords.

The soldiers of the Greek state of Sparta became very specialized by the seventh century B.C.E. Called hoplites, these foot soldiers received special training and wore protective bronze armor. Hoplites' armor was more flexible than earlier armor. Hoplites also wore bronze leg guards called greaves and bronze helmets with cheek guards that were decorated on top with plumed crests of horsehair, resembling a mohawk. They also carried bronze or leather shields with a long spear and a short sword.

These soldiers wear various styles of boots and armor traditionally found in Greek military dress. *Reproduced by permission of © Burstein Collection/CORBIS.*

FOR MORE INFORMATION

Chisholm, Jane, Lisa Miles, and Struan Reid. *The Usborne Encyclopedia of Ancient Greece.* London, England: Usborne Publishing, 1999.

■ Minoan Dress

The Minoans, who lived on the Greek island of Crete between 3000 and 1600 B.C.E., had a very complex culture, more advanced than many of the societies that followed it. This complexity is shown in the artistically designed and skillfully made clothing they wore. Much of our knowledge of this clothing comes from artwork that has been found at the sites where the Minoans lived, thousands of years before most recorded history.

The society of ancient Crete was largely unknown to modern people until the late 1800s C.E., when one of their ancient cities was discovered. Until that time most scholars thought that stories of a Cretan civilization ruled by a king named Minos were only legends. As historians began to study the ruins of the ancient Cretan city, they learned that the people who lived there had a richly developed culture with many similarities to modern societies. They called this culture Minoan, after the legendary King Minos in Greek mythology.

Minoans wore a variety of complex garments that were sewn together in very much the same way that modern garments are made. Unlike the classical Greeks who followed them hundreds of years later, the Minoans sewed skirts and blouses that were shaped to the body of the wearer. Crete is located in the southern Mediterranean and has a hot climate, so heavy clothes were not needed. Ancient Minoan men wore only loincloths, which were small pieces of fabric wrapped around the waist to cover the genitals. However, even these small garments were made with much attention to detail. Loincloths were made from a wide variety of materials, such as linen, leather, or wool, and decorated with bright colors and patterns. Many had a decorative pagne or sheath that covered and protected the penis, and some had long aprons in the front and back with tassels or fringe. While early Minoan men usually went bare-chested, in the later years of the Minoan civilization men often wore simple tunics and long robes.

The first modern scholars to study Crete were astonished by the design of the women's costume, including blouses and skirts that closely resembled modern women's clothing. Minoan women wore skirts that flared out from the waist in a bell shape, with many decorations attached to the cloth. Later designs were made from strips of fabric, sewn in ways that created rows of ruffles from waist to ankle. Women also wore close-fitting blouses that were cut low in the front to expose the breasts. A tiny waist was prized, and both men and women wore tight belts made of metal, which held their waists in. Some historians believe that these belts must have been worn since early childhood, forcing the waist to stop growing.

The figure of the Minoan woman, with large breasts, large hips, and tiny waist, was very similar to the female shape that came into fashion during the late 1800s C.E., when women laced themselves into tight corsets to make their waists small and wore hoops under their skirts to increase the size of their bottom half. Some experts believe that Minoan women must have also had some sort of framework under their skirts to support the bell shape. In fact, so close were Minoan fashions to popular French fashions of the 1800s that one of the women in an ancient Minoan painting was nicknamed "La Parisienne" (the woman of Paris) by those who discovered her.

FOR MORE INFORMATION

Bigelow, Marybelle S. *Fashion in History: Western Dress, Prehistoric to Present.* Minneapolis, MN: Burgess Publishing, 1970.

Payne, Blanche. *History of Costume: From Ancient Egypt to the 20th Century.* New York: Harper and Row, 1965.

[*See also* Volume 1, Ancient Greece: Loin Coverings; Volume 3, Eighteenth Century: Corsets]

Peplos

The peplos was a simple sleeveless outer garment worn by the women of ancient Greece up to the early part of the sixth century B.C.E. Like many Greek garments, the peplos was formed from one large rectangle of woven fabric, which was folded and pinned in specific ways to become a gracefully draped tunic-like cloak. Around 540 B.C.E. the peplos was replaced by the Ionic chiton, another type of tunic, as the most basic female garment, but the peplos continued to be represented in Greek art and literature as a symbol of the graceful simplicity of early Greek style.

The peplos was usually woven to order for each individual. Most peplos were made of wool, though some wealthy women had them made of fine linen or silk. Wealthier Greeks could afford to have their clothing dyed in bright colors and patterns; stripes and dot prints were popular for peplos. The garment was a long rectangle, from six to ten feet in width and usually one or two feet longer than the height of the wearer. When worn, the fabric was folded over at the top, so that about eighteen inches of fabric hung down, then the folded fabric was folded again lengthways to form a tube with one open side. The wearer stepped into the tube and secured the top at the shoulders with fibulae, fasteners that resemble safety pins, creating a garment with a sort of cape or overblouse.

When the Ionic chiton became a popular garment the peplos was worn as a cloak or overgarment over the chiton. It could be worn in different ways according to individual taste and style. The simplest method was to let the peplos hang loosely from the shoulders. However, it also became stylish to wear a belt or girdle, either under the folded fabric that hung down from the shoulders, or over it. Either way, the belt caused the fabric to fall in pleats and folds from the shoulder pins to the belt, then from the belt to the floor. Athenian women, from the ancient Greek city-state of Athens, usually sewed all or part of the open side of the peplos for the sake of modesty, but women from the ancient Greek city of Sparta wore their peplos open, shocking the rest of Greece by showing their thighs.

By the mid-sixth century B.C.E. the peplos lost favor. Artists began showing women and goddesses in other types of clothing, such as the elaborately draped Ionic chiton. The peplos was the forerunner to the Doric chiton, a wool tunic, of the fifth century B.C.E.

FOR MORE INFORMATION

Symons, David J. *Costume of Ancient Greece.* New York: Chelsea House, 1987.

[*See also* **Volume 1, Ancient Greece: Doric Chiton**]

Greek Headwear

Ancient Greek culture is divided among three general societies: Minoan, Mycenaean, and Greek. Each of these societies developed sophisticated civilizations, and the earlier societies influenced those that followed. In all, a variety of different ways of adorning the head were created.

In Minoan society, which developed on the Greek island of Crete about 3000 B.C.E., long hair was prized for both men and

A gold Mycenaean diadem. Diadems as well as wreaths and caps were often used to adorn the heads of both Greek men and women. *Reproduced by permission of © Wolfgang Kaehler/CORBIS.*

women. Frescoes, a form of paint applied directly to a wall's wet plaster, on palace walls and pictures on pottery show men and women with long, wavy black hair that reaches anywhere from the shoulders to below the buttocks. Men wore their long hair simply hanging down their backs and sometimes grew beards or mustaches. Some had short hair. Women wore elaborately styled long hairstyles. Paintings and pottery show women with sections of their hair waved or tied in an assortment of knots. Both men and women wore hats. Depictions of religious figures show women wearing three-tiered cone-like hats or flat hats with elaborate decorations on top, including statues of animals and feathers such as peacock plumes.

Mycenaean society, which developed on what is now the mainland of Greece, was greatly influenced by the Minoans who had developed on the island of Crete. Although the Minoan culture had waned at the time the Mycenaeans came to Crete, the Mycenaeans adopted much of the Minoan culture into their own. In the early years their hairstyles were similar to the Minoans but much more carefully styled in long curls held in place by richly decorated diadems, or crowns, and ribbons. Later, perhaps for convenience as they entered into a number of wars, Mycenaean men cut their hair short or bound it closely to their head and grew beards.

After the fall of the Minoan and Mycenaean civilizations in about 1200 B.C.E., Greek society developed. To the Greeks hair was a beautiful, important fashion accessory, and they created many hair accessories and styles. In the early years of Greek society both men and women wore their hair long, usually tied with a headband. Greeks living in the area called Sparta, in the central part of Greece, regarded their long hair as bestowing them with special powers and strength. To achieve the most beautiful styles, wigs and other hairpieces were worn by both men and women. Greeks also found it fashionable to darken their gray hair or dye their hair blond. To lighten their hair, Greeks washed their hair in potash, made from wood ashes, soaked it in yellow flowers, and dried it in the sun. Oils were also applied to the hair to make it shine.

As the society developed over hundreds of years, Greek hairstyles became more restrained. Men and women would twist and tie up their hair with bands. For special occasions, women adorned their heads with decorative metal bands called stephane, which looked much like modern-day tiaras. By the early fourth century B.C.E., women often covered their bound-up hair with scarves called sphendone or caps such as the sakkos, a soft woven cap with a tassel hanging from the center or a piece of material wrapped around the head.

Starting in the sixth century B.C.E. men more and more commonly wore their hair short until the Greek ruler Alexander the Great (356–323 B.C.E.) returned the fashion of longer hair in the fourth century B.C.E. Men again began cutting their hair short in the third century and continued to wear short hair until the end of Greek rule in 146 B.C.E. Popular styles included short curls and curls combed away from the face.

For most of early Greek life Greek men could decide whether or not they wished to wear beards or mustaches as a matter of personal taste. Beards could be worn full, pointed, or closely cropped, with a mustache or without. However, Alexander the Great popularized the look of clean-shaven skin, and fewer and fewer men wore beards after his reign.

Greek men wore hats for functional purposes, not fashionable ones. The pilos, petasos, and Phrygian caps were worn for work or travel by farmers, soldiers, and travelers. Decorative headgear included wreaths made of natural branches or golden ornaments that were worn for special occasions and to signify great honors.

FOR MORE INFORMATION

Batterberry, Michael, and Ariane Batterberry. *Fashion: The Mirror of History.* New York: Greenwich House, 1982.

Corson, Richard. *Fashions in Hair: The First Five Thousand Years.* London, England: Peter Owen, 2001.

Symons, David J. *Costume of Ancient Greece.* New York: Chelsea House, 1987.

Trasko, Mary. *Daring Do's: A History of Extraordinary Hair.* New York: Flammarion, 1994.

Phrygian Cap

A hood-like hat with a pointed top, the Phrygian cap was introduced to ancient Greece around 500 B.C.E. from the nearby

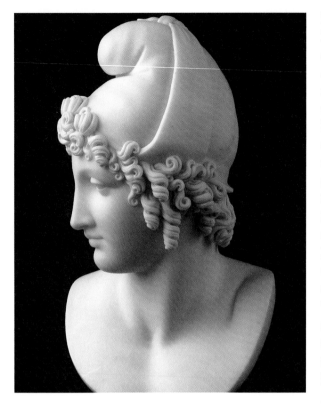

A Greek man wearing a Phrygian cap. *Reproduced by permission of © Araldo de Luca/CORBIS.*

land of Phrygia, in what is now Turkey. The Phrygian people of the sixth and seventh centuries B.C.E. had many influences on ancient Greek culture, among them a tight-fitting cap with a pointed top which angled to the front. The Phrygian cap is brimless, but may have flaps over or in front of the ears, and also sometimes has a long flap in the back to protect the neck. The caps were sometimes made of stiffened fabric or leather, which made it sit up on the head like a helmet, with the pointed top curving towards the front of the head. Other Phrygian caps were made of soft felt, with the point either flattened onto the crown of the cap, hung to the side, or stood up softly. The Phrygian cap was later popular during several different time periods and has been seen on a wide variety of people from French revolutionaries of 1789 to the seven dwarves in Walt Disney's *Snow White and the Seven Dwarfs* (1937). The style is still echoed in some types of modern stocking caps.

The Phrygian cap became popular wear for many Greek men, from soldiers to farmers, and the style continued to spread after Greece was conquered by the Roman Empire in 146 B.C.E. Men continued to wear Phrygian caps at various times throughout the Middle Ages (c. 500–c. 1500 C.E.), and they rose to tremendous popularity again during the French Revolution, which began in 1789. An ancient Roman custom of giving Phrygian caps to slaves who gained their freedom inspired French revolutionaries to adopt the cap, which they dubbed the "liberty cap." The soft felt cap was dashing enough for freedom fighters, yet simple enough to provide a contrast with the stiff three-cornered, or tricorne, hats of the aristocracy. The Phrygian cap, often made from red cloth, became the symbol of French liberty.

Phrygian caps have continued to be symbols of freedom, and pictures of them are often found on official seals and banners, such as the state seal of West Virginia, the presidential flag of Argentina, and the Treasury seal of Paraguay. A 1992 song by the rock group

XTC, "Then She Appeared," describes a woman who appears "Dressed in tricolour [the French flag] and Phrygian cap."

FOR MORE INFORMATION

Cosgrave, Bronwyn. *The Complete History of Costume and Fashion: From Ancient Egypt to the Present Day.* New York: Checkmark Books, 2000.

Sichel, Marion. *Costume of the Classical World.* New York: Chelsea House, 1980.

Pilos and Petasos

The two most common hats worn in Greece from 1200 to 146 B.C.E. were the pilos (PEE-loss) and the petasos (PEH-ta-sus). Felt, a smooth cloth, was the most common material used to make the hats, but other materials were also used, including leather and straw. Evidence of many different felt hats formed into a cone shape with a small rolled brim has been discovered in many regions of Greece. These hats were worn by working men. In each region, the hats were usually named after the geographic area in which they were worn. Scholars, however, have not been able to distinguish differences among these many different regional hats and have come to call all these felt hats with little brims pilos. The Greek god of fire and metalworking, Hephaestus, is often depicted wearing a pilos.

A larger hat, known as the petasos, protected Greeks from the rain and the heat of the sun, especially when traveling. The petasos was a low-crowned, wide-brimmed hat with a strap to secure it on the wearer's head or to hang it down the wearer's back until needed. The brim of the petasos could be shaped into several different forms. The earliest petasos had upturned brims in the back; later versions had brims cut into decorative shapes. The origin of the petasos is believed to be the Greek region of Thessaly.

The popularity of both the pilos and the petasos spread to other cultures. From 750 B.C.E. to 200 B.C.E. Etruscan men, from the area now comprising central Italy, wore these hats that had been developed by the Greeks. Later, from 509 B.C.E. to 476 C.E., Roman men also wore hats resembling the Greek pilos and petasos. Serbian hatmakers continued making these hats until just before World War II (1939–45) by rubbing soaked wool fibers together between their palms and shaping them into close-fitting felt hats.

FOR MORE INFORMATION

Payne, Blanche, Geitel Winakor, and Jane Farrell-Beck. *The History of Costume: From Ancient Mesopotamia Through the Twentieth Century.* 2nd ed. New York: HarperCollins, 1992.

Symons, David J. *Costume of Ancient Greece.* New York: Chelsea House, 1987.

Sakkos and Sphendone

Greek women covered their heads in a variety of ways starting in 500 B.C.E. Evidence of their headwear has been found on sculptures and in writings from the period. A type of cap called a sakkos was worn by many. The sakkos could be a soft woven cap with a tassel hanging from the center or a piece of material wrapped around the head. In either case the sakkos completely covered the hair, which was tied into a bun, except for the bangs or curls by the ears. Sometimes women wore a stephane, a metal upturned headband much like a tiara, as a decorative brim for their sakkos. A smaller sakkos, called a sphendone, was a scarf wound around the head that covered the lower portion of the bun in back but exposed the bun's top. The sakkos and sphendone fell out of fashion starting in about 330 B.C.E. At this time women continued to wear their hair tied up but no longer covered it with scarves or hats.

FOR MORE INFORMATION

Symons, David J. *Costume of Ancient Greece.* New York: Chelsea House, 1987.

Wreaths

Wreaths are circular decorations usually made of flowers, vines, leaves, or other materials fashioned in the shape of leaves or flowers. In modern times wreaths have most often been used as a household decoration, displayed on a table or hung on a door. However, in ancient Greece, beginning around the sixth century B.C.E., wreaths were a common personal adorn-ment. Worn on the head as a sort of crown, wreaths not only served as decoration but often indicated a great honor, such as a victory in war or an achievement in work or study. Since ancient times wreaths have also been used to honor the dead.

In ancient Greece peo-ple felt their connection with nature deeply, and nature was given importance in the reli-gions of the day. For the Greeks of around 500 B.C.E., many flowers and plants had special meanings, and often gods and goddesses were iden-tified with certain plants.

A man wearing wreath. Wreaths could be made of flowers, vines, or leaves and often indicated a great honor, such as a victory in war or an achievement in work or study. *Reproduced by permission of © Elio Ciol/CORBIS.*

Therefore, the wearing of plants had a certain significance. Though women did weave some flowers and leaves into wreaths to wear in their hair as simple decoration, other wreaths were only worn on certain special occasions. For example, those who celebrated the wild rites of Dionysus, the god of wine and merrymaking, often wore wreaths of grape leaves and ivy. Leaves of the grapevine were also used to make the wreaths worn by actors who performed in the fa-mous Greek theaters, and laurel wreaths were placed on the heads of poets and scholars who were honored for their work.

Another occasion that called for wreaths was athletic competition. The most famous of these were the Olympic games, which were held every four years in the city of Olympia in honor of Zeus, the most powerful of the Greek gods. Young men came from all over Greece to compete in the games, and winners were honored with crowns of olive leaves. There were other games around Greece, and each had its own particular wreath. Winners of the Pythian games, which honored the god Apollo, received wreaths of laurel, which was sacred to the god. The Isthmian games, held in the city of Isthmia, featured victory wreaths made of pine needles, while the Nemean games, held in Nemea, a valley northwest of Argos, offered leaves of wild parsley.

Victorious generals were crowned with wreaths, as were priests and priestesses performing religious rituals. Along with living heroes the Greeks also adorned statues of gods, goddesses, and famous mortals with wreaths. An olive wreath hung on a Greek door during the fifth or sixth centuries B.C.E. announced the birth of a baby boy. It was fashionable at the time for Greek women to adorn their hair with elaborate jewelry, and some wore wreaths made of gold leaves.

FOR MORE INFORMATION

Norris, Herbert. *Costume and Fashion: The Evolution of European Dress Through the Earlier Ages.* London, England: J. M. Dent and Sons, 1924. Reprint, New York: E. P. Dutton, 1931.

Greek Body Decorations

The early Greeks were very concerned about their physical appearance and celebrated the human form. The depictions of Minoans living on the Greek island of Crete and Mycenaeans living on the Greek mainland from 3000 to 1200 B.C.E. indicate these cultures idealized the human figure. Both men and women are drawn with slim figures, tiny waists encircled by metal girdles, and flowing black hair. With the exception of the tiny waists, ancients Greeks living from 800 to 146 B.C.E. held the human body in similar esteem. Greeks, especially those living in the state of Sparta, in central Greece, exercised regularly to keep their minds and bodies fit.

To prepare the body for dress, Greeks bathed every day, scrubbing with pumice stones to remove unwanted hair and make the skin smooth. Both men and women also rubbed perfumed oil over their skin to make their skin gleam.

To complement their elaborately wrapped garments and carefully styled hair, Greek women adorned themselves with rings, necklaces, bracelets, earrings, and hair ornaments made of precious metals and decorated with gemstones. Women also used white lead or chalk to hide imperfections on their faces, brushed rouge, or a reddish powder, on their cheeks, and outlined their eyes with eye paint. Men did not wear makeup but wore rings and used decorative fibulae (pins) to clasp their cloaks and chitons (tunics).

FOR MORE INFORMATION

Chisholm, Jane, Lisa Miles, and Struan Reid. *The Usborne Encyclopedia of Ancient Greece*. London, England: Usborne Publishing, 1999.

Payne, Blanche, Geitel Winakor, and Jane Farrell-Beck. *The History of Costume: From Ancient Mesopotamia Through the Twentieth Century*. 2nd ed. New York: HarperCollins, 1992.

Symons, David J. *Costume of Ancient Greece.* New York: Chelsea House, 1987.

Cameo and Intaglio

Engraving stones for use as jewelry had been a highly prized art in early Assyrian (one of the great ancient empires of southeast Asia) and Egyptian cultures but only began to be developed in Greece in the sixth century B.C.E. The first method of engraving used by the Greeks was known as intaglio, or cutting a design into the surface of a stone. Intaglios, especially those on signet rings, were used as signatures by stamping impressions of the design into wax or other substances. Later, in the fourth century B.C.E., engravers perfected a method of creating raised designs on stones, called cameo.

The Greeks engraved designs into a variety of precious stones, such as onyx, sardonyx, agate, cornelian, sard, chalcedony, jasper, and lapis lazuli, as well as gems, such as emerald, sapphire, ruby, and garnet. Once engraved, these stones were set in delicately engraved and carefully shaped precious metals, such as gold.

Later cultures also developed methods of both intaglio and cameo engraving. Roman jewelers in the first century C.E. made intricate wedding rings with carvings of the heads of the bride and groom and delicate pendants. Rich citizens of the Byzantine Empire of the fourth through the fifteenth centuries C.E. wore cameo rings and other elaborate jewelry. Cameo brooches or pins with medallions of profiled heads were especially popular among European women in the late eighteenth and early nineteenth centuries.

FOR MORE INFORMATION

Payne, Blanche, Geitel Winakor, and Jane Farrell-Beck. *The History of Costume: From Ancient Mesopotamia Through the Twentieth Century.* 2nd ed. New York: HarperCollins, 1992.

[*See also* **Volume 3, Eighteenth Century: Cameo**]

Fibulae

Ancient Greeks fastened their clothes with fibulae. Fibulae, which resembled safety pins, secured the large panels of fabric that Greeks draped around their bodies. Although they began as a necessity for holding clothing in place, fibulae later became decorative fashion items.

The first fibulae were carved from the leg bones of birds, which some scholars believe to be the source of the pins' name since fibula is also the name used for a particular leg bone. The earliest metal fibulae date back to about 1000 B.C.E. These unadorned fibulae were made of bronze or gold and looked very similar to modern safety pins.

As Greek goldsmiths became more skilled in their craft from 480 to 336 B.C.E., they created more elaborate, decorative fibulae.

A variety of silver fibulae, which were used to fasten robes and other clothing in ancient Greece. *Reproduced by permission of © Archivo Iconografico, S.A./ CORBIS.*

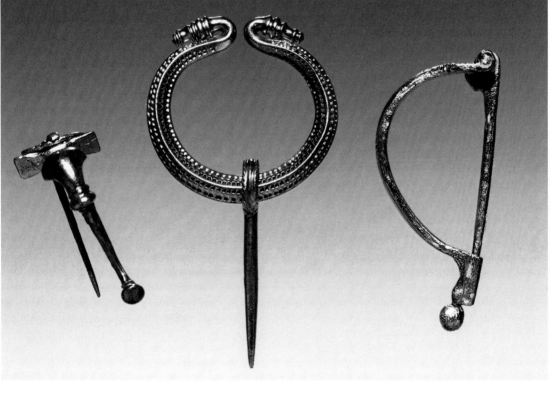

Examples of fibulae from this time have beautifully wrought golden designs. By the fall of the Greek Empire around 146 B.C.E., fibulae were quite beautiful and worn with less-functional jewelry pieces to adorn Greek garments.

Later cultures continued to make and use fibulae. Etruscans, from the area now comprising central Italy, made glass beads to decorate fibulae between 750 B.C.E. and 200 B.C.E. Fibulae were one of the main types of jewelry worn by Roman men and were prized clasps for military cloaks between 509 B.C.E. and 476 C.E. Fibulae were also worn by Roman women. After the decline of the Roman Empire, the Byzantines ruled a rich and powerful empire in central Europe, Italy, and part of Asia from 330 to 1095 C.E. Byzantines considered jeweled fibulae fashionable clasps for men's cloaks. By the eleventh century, as the ancient empires declined, more primitive groups of nomadic tribes in central Europe wore simple metal fibulae.

FOR MORE INFORMATION

Payne, Blanche, Geitel Winakor, and Jane Farrell-Beck. *The History of Costume: From Ancient Mesopotamia Through the Twentieth Century.* 2nd ed. New York: HarperCollins, 1992.

▪ Jewelry

During the high point of ancient Greek civilization, from about 600 B.C.E. to 146 B.C.E., Greek men and women set a precedent for the wearing of personal ornaments that has continued in the Western world up to the present day. The first pieces of jewelry in Greek society were not purely ornamental, but instead they had specific functions, such as a pin to secure a garment or a band to manage the hair. These functional pieces were later embellished to become decorative and pleasing to the wearer.

Although blacksmiths made objects out of gold, silver, and bronze before the third century B.C.E., Greek goldsmiths after this date became very skillful at creating intricately designed ornaments for both men and women to wear. The skills of the goldsmiths increased people's desire for jewelry made for purely decorative reasons.

Some of the earliest jewelry were thin metal plates embossed, or ornamented with raised work, with designs and trimmed with raised metal beads or twisted golden wire, as well as elaborate creations made of gold wire, sometimes featuring beads, that became known as filigree. From 336 to 323 B.C.E. Macedonian king Alexander the Great (356–323 B.C.E.), ruler of the Greek people at the time, traveled extensively and brought back precious gemstones from Asia, including rubies, topazes, emeralds, opals, pearls, and diamonds. Soon jewelers incorporated these stones into jewelry.

Earrings appeared for the first time in Greece in 900 B.C.E. These first earrings were golden or bronze hoops, which soon became larger and more elaborate designs of hanging gold balls or nearly four-inch-long vase-shaped ornaments. By 600 B.C.E. multipieced earrings were worn. These included small coin-shaped pieces that hung on chains from a central larger disc and made a pleasant noise as the wearer moved. During the reign of Alexander the Great earrings became even more elaborate and included designs with dangling figurines and golden flower baskets. The earliest gems to be used in earrings in Greece were pearls. Pear-shaped pearls were especially popular. Two earrings were popular for adult women, but fashionable Greek youths often wore a single earring.

A pair of gold earrings from around 150 B.C.E. Usually only the wealthiest in Greek society could afford to wear gold jewelry. *Reproduced by permission of © Christie's Images/CORBIS.*

Necklaces and bracelets were also popular. Amber beads or pearls were often strung around the neck. Another popular necklace design featured chains with golden disc or ball ornaments with attached rings or short chains that dangled other ornaments. The bracelet style seen most often was of a gold, silver, or bronze wire twisted around the arm imitating a snake. Jewelry styles similar to those of the ancient Greeks continue to be worn by fashionable women around the world.

FOR MORE INFORMATION

Cosgrave, Bronwyn. *The Complete History of Costume and Fashion, from Ancient Egypt to the Present Day.* New York: Checkmark Books, 2000.

Norris, Herbert. *Costume and Fashion: The Evolution of European Dress Through the Earlier Ages.* London, England: J. M. Dent and Sons, 1924. Reprint, New York: E. P. Dutton, 1931.

Makeup

Greek women embraced the use of makeup to enhance their beauty. Evidence of how females made up their faces can be found in such different places as on palace frescos, paintings directly on the wall, from Knossos, the royal city on the ancient Greek island of Crete, dating back to 1500 B.C.E. and in the descriptive poems written during the Greek Classical Period from 500 to 336 B.C.E. Although the practice was limited to women of wealth and influence, probably because of the cost, makeup was an important part of fashion in ancient Greece.

In the sunny climate of ancient Greece, noblewomen, especially those living in Athens, the cultural center of Greece, tried to keep their skin pale. Women smoothed a paste of white lead mixed with water over their faces, necks, shoulders, and arms to create a wrinkle-free, white appearance. Another cosmetic preparation involved soaking white lead in vinegar, collecting the corroded portion, grinding it into a powder, and then heating it.

Women then applied brightly colored lipstick and rouge, or reddish powder, made from a variety of materials such as seaweed, flowers, or crushed mulberries. Dark eye shadow, eyeliner, and eyebrow coloring was made from soot. Greeks used their makeup boldly, drawing red circles or other designs with rouge on their cheeks and accenting their eyebrows and eyes with dark outlines and sweeping lines.

Greek women were so heavily made-up that their carefully crafted faces were in danger of washing away with sweat. The poet Eubulus, in his circa 360 B.C.E. comedy *The Wreath-Sellers,* vividly described the threat of Greece's climate to women in Athens: "If you go out when it is hot, two streams of black make-up flow from your eyebrows, and red stripes run from your cheeks to your neck. The hair hanging down on to the forehead is matted with white lead." Eubulus's description suggests that when Greek women wore makeup they tried to protect themselves from the heat of the sun, perhaps by staying inside.

FOR MORE INFORMATION

Gröning, Karl. *Body Decoration: A World Survey of Body Art.* New York: Vendome Press, 1998.

Symons, David J. *Costume of Ancient Greece.* New York: Chelsea House, 1987.

[*See also* **Volume 1, Ancient Rome: Makeup; Volume 4, 1919–29: Makeup; Volume 5, 1946–60: Makeup**]

Metal Girdles

Long before the term "girdle" was used to describe a tight, corset-like garment worn by women to make their waists appear slim, a girdle was a kind of belt or sash, tied or wrapped around the waist. The word "gird" means to encircle, or go around, and girdles encircled the wearer. In ancient times the girdle was a very useful part of many costumes, holding long, draped garments or short, loose outfits in place. Girdles were also decorative and could be a kind of jewelry for the waist. Girdles were often made of cloth but were sometimes made of metal, decorated with precious stones and beads. The ancient Egyptians were among the first to develop metalworking skills, and they used these skills to make jewelry as early as 2700 B.C.E. The societies of the Greek island of Crete, from around 2000 B.C.E., and those of Hellenic Greece (the period before Alexander the Great [356–323 B.C.E.]), from around 800 B.C.E., also learned the art of metalwork, and they made decorative metal girdles an important part of their fashionable dress.

The Greek island of Crete was home to a flourishing civilization from about 3000 B.C.E. This civilization was named Minoan after King Minos, a legendary king in Greek mythology. Most modern knowledge of Minoan culture comes from the art that has been found by later generations. This art shows that the Minoans were fine metalworkers. Much Minoan art seems to indicate Minoans found a tiny waist attractive. In order to make the shoulders and

A Minoan woman wearing a metal girdle around her waist. Metal girdles were often worn from a young age to restrict growth and to keep the waist small. *Reproduced by permission of © Wolfgang Kaehler/CORBIS.*

chest appear larger and stronger, Minoan men and women pulled their waists in with tight belts, often made of metals such as copper, silver, and gold. These belts were rolled at the edges and decorated with designs of ridges, spirals, rosettes, and flowers. Experts believe that in many cases these decorated metal belts were welded permanently around the waists of small children in order to keep the waist small as the child grew up. Some experts think that the Minoan metal belts might have had religious importance, since metal girdles shaped like snakes have been found in Minoan temples. Other researchers believe that this practice of tightening the waist may have been more than simple fashion. They think the custom may have come from a time when Minoans depended on the uncertain luck of hunting for survival, and a small stomach could be a practical necessity when food was scarce.

Later Greek cultures were influenced by the metalworking techniques of both the Egyptians and the Minoans, and they also loved to adorn themselves with jewelry, including decorative metal girdles. In their mythology, too, the girdle had special significance. In Greek myth the famous hero Heracles, also known as Hercules, was sent on a quest to steal the golden girdle of the Queen of the Amazons, because whoever wore it would have great power. The magic jeweled girdle of the love goddess Aphrodite was supposed to have the power to make people fall in love with anyone who wore it.

Thousands of years later, girdles and their ancestors are still used to shape women's bodies. The corset, similar to a girdle in the way it shapes the body, was popular from the sixteenth to the nineteenth centuries, and supermodels of the late twentieth century were known to wear a tight belt under their clothes to keep from eating.

FOR MORE INFORMATION

Houston, Mary G. *Ancient Greek, Roman, and Byzantine Costume and Decoration.* Lanham, MD: Barnes and Noble Books-Imports, 1977.

Symons, David. *Costume of Ancient Greece.* Broomall, PA: Chelsea House Publishers, 1988.

[*See also* **Volume 3, Eighteenth Century: Corsets**]

Perfume

Smelling good was of great concern to the ancient Greeks. But without running water, their techniques for freshening themselves were different than modern methods of bathing and showering. Men and women washed themselves with a cloth and a bowl of water or by rubbing olive oil on their skin, scraping it off with a metal rod called a strigil, and rinsing with cold water. Once clean, Greeks would apply perfumes all over their skin and hair.

To make perfume Greeks soaked spices and other fragrant flowers and herbs in warm oil until the oil took on a pleasant scent. They would then strain the ingredients from the oil and use the perfumed oil alone or mix it with a sticky gum to make a thicker perfumed cream. Cinnamon, basil, marjoram, almonds, roses, lavender, and lilies were popular fragrances for perfume. Greeks kept their perfume in beautifully decorated glass or ceramic bottles or carved alabaster vials hung as pendants from chains around their necks.

FOR MORE INFORMATION

Crosher, Judith. *Technology in the Time of Ancient Greece.* Austin, TX: Raintree Steck-Vaughn, 1998.

Symons, David J. *Costume of Ancient Greece.* New York: Chelsea House, 1987.

Greek Footwear

Early Minoan and Mycenaean men and women living between about 3000 B.C.E. and 1200 B.C.E. mostly went barefoot, but they did have a variety of sandals, shoes, and boots for outdoor wear. Early Greeks living between about 800 B.C.E. and 146 B.C.E. followed this tradition as well. All classes of Greeks went barefoot when indoors, removing their shoes when entering a house or temple. The proof of these practices has been discovered by archeologists, scientists who study the physical remains of the past. They have found that the outside steps of palaces and temples are far more worn down than the indoor steps, indicating that shoes were not worn indoors. Even outdoors, however, many children, slaves, and those who could not afford them wore no shoes. The Spartans, mainland Greeks who were famous for being great warriors, prided themselves on the toughness they showed by never wearing shoes. As shoemaking became a more developed craft, and shoes became more useful and comfortable, more and more Greeks began to wear them.

Footwear of all sorts was made mostly of leather, and occasionally of felt, or smooth cloth, or wood. Greeks tanned the hides of cattle for the majority of their footwear and developed a process known as tawing to cure the softer hides of calves, sheep, and goats for the finest shoes. Tawing produced soft white leather shoes. Tanned hides were a natural tan color but were sometimes dyed black, red, or yellow. For the very wealthy, shoes could be gilded, or coated in gold.

Footwear came in an abundance of styles. Styles were named after the place of origin, the famous people who made the style fashionable, as well as an assortment of specific names for certain styles. Greeks identified with their footwear so much that some people were given the nickname of their favorite shoe style.

FOR MORE INFORMATION

Batterberry, Michael, and Ariane Batterberry. *Fashion: The Mirror of History*. New York: Greenwich House, 1982.

Symons, David J. *Costume of Ancient Greece*. New York: Chelsea House, 1987.

Boots

Boots, shoes that cover part of the leg as well as the foot, have been worn to protect the feet and legs since very ancient times. The people of ancient Greece, beginning with the Minoans from the Greek island of Crete dating from 3000 to 1400 B.C.E., made many different styles of boots and developed shoemaking into a skilled craft and a fine art.

The ancient Greek society of Minoans, named for a legendary king in Greek mythology, Minos, had a highly developed sense of decorative fashion. Along with colorful skirts and tunics, they wore many types of slippers, shoes, and boots. Though most historians believe that shoes were not worn indoors, many Cretans did wear boots outside. Women wore delicate ankle boots as well as tall boots with high heels, and Cretan men wore tall boots that covered the calf and were tied on with leather straps. Young Minoan men and women played a special athletic game where they performed gymnastic stunts over the backs of running bulls. For these ritual games, they wore special knee-high boots of leather dyed tan, red, or white.

Later, in the classical Greek society of the fifth and sixth centuries B.C.E., almost all Greeks went barefoot much of the time. Shoes were never worn inside, and even the wealthiest people only wore sandals outdoors. However, those who did heavy outdoor work, such as soldiers, farmers, hunters, and some slaves, often wore boots rather than sandals. Ancient Greek boots resembled sandals in many ways. Many were tied on with leather straps like sandals, and some covered the sole, sides of the foot, and calf, while leaving the toes and the top of the foot bare. Some young Greek men wore leggings that resembled boot tops but left their feet bare. Soldiers often wore high boots with wooden soles and leather tops, which were tied on with wide leather laces. Other Greek boots had leather or felt soles that laced up the front like modern shoes and tied at the ankle or the calf. By the end of the fifth century B.C.E. many young men wore highly decorated boots made of white leather or fabric, with turned down tops trimmed in bright colors.

The stage actors who performed the famous Greek dramatic plays also wore boots. Different styles of boot were used to help the audience distinguish the characters. For example, since all ancient Greek actors were men, the actors who portrayed female characters often wore loose-fitting boots, while the actors who played the male characters wore tightly laced boots to help the audience distinguish the men from the women in the play.

FOR MORE INFORMATION

Kippen, Cameron. "The History of Footwear: Sandals." *Curtin University of Technology Department of Podiatry.* http://podiatry.curtin.edu.au/ sandal.html (accessed on July 24, 2003).

Payne, Blanche, Geitel Winakor, and Jane Farrell-Beck. *The History of Costume: From Ancient Mesopotamia Through the Twentieth Century.* 2nd ed. New York: HarperCollins, 1992.

Sandals

Sandals are simple footwear composed of a sole that is held onto the foot by straps. Though the ancient Greeks did not invent the style, they did create many types of leather sandals, developing shoemaking into a skilled art and introducing a wide variety of footwear styles for all classes of men and women. By 500 B.C.E. the average Greek citizen could tell much about the people that passed in the street by the style of sandals they wore.

Early Greek sandals were made from a stiff leather or wooden sole to which leather straps were attached. These straps usually went between the wearer's big toe and second toe and around the back of the ankle to hold the sole firmly to the bottom of the foot. Much of the individual design of these sandals was created by the different ways the leather straps wrapped around the foot and ankle. Wealthy people wore soft leather sandals, sometimes dyed in various colors. The very wealthy sometimes even had gilded sandals, or

Greek men wearing different types of sandals. Sandals were worn to protect the feet against the elements as well as for style and to pronounce social status.
Reproduced by permission of © Bettmann/CORBIS.

sandals painted gold, in which the leather was covered with real gold. Some high officials and stage actors wore sandals called buskins, with tall soles made of cork, which made them appear taller. Some shoemakers carved designs or placed nails in the soles of their sandals in various patterns, so that the footprints of the wearer left a distinctive mark. One pair of ancient Greek sandals has been found that left the words "Follow me," written in every footprint, and many experts believe that the shoes must have belonged to a prostitute. Workers wore heavy-duty sandals, such as the thick leather crepida, which were made with an extra-large sole and wrapped around to protect the sides of the foot, then laced up the top.

Shoemakers became respected citizens in the Greece of the fourth and fifth centuries B.C.E., and their craft was believed to be watched over by the god Apollo—god of the sun, music, poetry, and healing, among others. Sandals themselves were sometimes given magical powers in the myths of the time. Though the gods and goddesses were often pictured barefoot, Hermes and Iris, the messengers of the gods, were always pictured in winged sandals, and goddesses such as Hera, the queen of the gods, and Aphrodite, goddess of love and beauty, were often depicted in golden sandals.

FOR MORE INFORMATION

Kippen, Cameron. "The History of Footwear: Sandals." *Curtin University of Technology Department of Podiatry.* http://podiatry.curtin.edu.au/ sandal.html (accessed on July 11, 2003).

Laver, James. *Costume and Fashion: A Concise History.* New York: Thames and Hudson, 2002.

Ancient Rome

The most powerful of the ancient empires, the civilization that became the Roman Empire rose from humble origins as a city in central Italy. At the height of its power, the Roman Empire stretched from Spain in the west to present-day Syria in the east, and from Egypt in the south to Britain in the north. The story of the rise and fall of the Roman Empire, including what the Romans wore during this fascinating era, has captivated historians for two thousand years.

From city to empire

Legend has it that the city of Rome was founded in 753 B.C.E. by Romulus and Remus, the twin sons of the god Mars, who had been raised by wolves. They established a small town that grew, over time, into a small city that controlled the surrounding region. Rome was one of many small city-states on the Italian peninsula. The most powerful of these city-states was inhabited by the Etruscans, who dominated most of Italy from about 800 B.C.E. until they finally were defeated by the Romans in 250 B.C.E. These small cities, and especially the Etruscans, had a great influence on the developing Roman civilization. Many of the cultural and costume traditions of the Romans were borrowed from the Etruscans.

A Roman amphitheater. Romans often put on plays, which entertained, educated, and displayed a variety of clothing styles. *Reproduced by permission of © Adam Woolfitt/CORBIS.*

Initially ruled by a king, in 509 B.C.E. the powerful families of Rome took control of the city-state and established it as a republic, with representatives of the citizens of the city choosing people to form a ruling senate. This began a long period of Roman history known as the Roman Republic (509–27 B.C.E.). At first only the wealthiest members of Roman society could join the government, but over time more of the poorer citizens, called plebeians, gained access to power. It was not a perfect democracy, but many people had the right to vote and thus to call themselves citizens. During the republic the Romans grew more powerful, and slowly they extended their rule. First they took control of much of the Italian peninsula, and then they extended their control into present-day Greece, Spain, and northern Africa. But the rise of powerful armies and the problems with managing an expanding society brought the republic many troubles that were soon addressed by a change in government.

In 27 B.C.E. a new era in Roman history began when a powerful general established himself as the first Roman emperor, thus beginning a period known as the Roman Empire (27 B.C.E.–476 C.E.). This emperor, Augustus (63 B.C.E.–14 C.E.), took full control of the empire, and he ruled over an era known as the Pax Romana, or Roman peace. For nearly two hundred years the empire flourished. New cities were created and trade with other societies expanded. The empire as a whole grew very rich. Conflict between the rulers of different cities, each with their own armies, soon began to tear the empire apart in a long civil war. The emperor Diocletian (c. 245–c. 316) reorganized the empire in 293 C.E., creating a Western Roman Empire centered in Rome and an Eastern Roman Empire centered in modern-day Turkey. These were united in 324 C.E. under an emperor known as Constantine the Great (c. 285–337 C.E.), yet even Constantine could not hold the empire together. The Western Empire slowly crumbled, attacked by armies from outside and beset by economic trouble from within, and ended in 476 C.E. The Eastern Roman Empire survived, however, as the Byzantine Empire, which lasted until 1453 C.E.

Triumphs and excesses of the empire

The great power that the Roman Empire held in the ancient world led to many accomplishments. Romans build a vast system of roadways and waterways that connected Europe and parts of the Middle East. They created a system of republican government, in which power lies with a group of citizens versus a supreme ruler, which lasted for several hundred years. And they established trade networks that stretched throughout the world, including a thriving trade with China and the Far East. Yet the great successes of Rome also brought troubling changes. The once sparing and simple Romans became lovers of luxury. The rulers had such great power and wealth that they felt anything was possible. The legend that the third-century-B.C.E. emperor Nero played his fiddle while the city of Rome burned has become a symbol for an uncaring ruler. The vicious combat that occurred in the arenas of Rome among gladiators—soldiers who fought to the death as public entertainment for ancient Romans—also showed a lack of concern for human life. Rome's leaders lost the support of their citizens, and eventually the empire could not hold together.

These larger historical changes can be seen in the way that Romans dressed and decorated themselves. Over the entire history of Roman civilization, a few garments provided the basis for the

SUMPTUARY LAWS REGULATE LUXURY

The early Romans, who founded their first city in Rome in 753 B.C.E., were a hard-working, serious people. They respected their elders and their family and were simple and frugal in their tastes, including their tastes in clothes. Over several hundred years they built a strong, well-ordered society. After 509 B.C.E., their society, known as the Roman Republic, controlled much of present-day Italy and was a rising power in the Mediterranean. But with rising power came problems.

The republic was governed by a senate that consisted of elected members from a small group of established wealthy families. As the Roman Republic became more powerful, more and more Romans had access to money. They used this money to buy colorful clothes and gold jewelry, and to throw lavish parties. The ruling families of the republic did not like the way these people displayed their wealth. They felt that proper Romans should behave just as the ruling families and their ancestors had behaved. So, beginning in about 215 B.C.E., Roman senators began to make laws to limit the ways people could dress and entertain themselves. These were called sumptuary laws because they related to personal expenditures.

This first Roman sumptuary law was called the Lex Appia. It declared that no woman could possess more than a half ounce of gold, wear a stola, or dress, of different colors, or ride in a carriage in any city unless for a public ceremony. Many other sumptuary laws followed. Laws were passed that listed how many different colors could be worn by members of different social classes: peasants could wear one color, soldiers in the army could wear two colors, army officers could wear three colors, and members of the royal family could wear seven

colors. A law passed by Emperor Aurelian, who ruled from 270 to 275 C.E., stated that men couldn't wear shoes that were red, yellow, green, or white, and that only the emperor and his sons could wear red or purple shoes. Under Aurelian, only ambassadors could wear gold rings and men were forbidden to wear silk. A variety of other laws limited how much people could spend on parties and how many people they could invite. Some of the laws seemed very silly.

Many people resented these sumptuary laws. They felt that the ruling class was trying to keep people from enjoying the benefits of their wealth. The ruling class, however, felt that open displays of wealth challenged their authority and upset the social order.

The Romans were not the first or the last to pass sumptuary laws. The ancient Greeks passed laws limiting how much gold a person could possess, as well as how people could entertain themselves. From the Middle Ages (c. 500–c. 1500 C.E.) through the nineteenth century, European monarchs passed sumptuary laws, often to restrict members of their courts and mere commoners from dressing in clothing that was more lavish than that worn by the king or queen. And Puritans in colonial Massachusetts, among the first European settlers in the American colonies, passed laws to keep people from wearing fancy clothes. They did not want common people to be mistaken for wealthier gentlemen.

No matter when they existed, sumptuary laws were designed to keep the social order from changing and to keep certain people from dressing like or entertaining themselves like wealthier or more powerful members of the society. For the most part, sumptuary laws don't exist in modern democratic countries, though some, like school dress codes some might argue, continue to this day.

Roman wardrobe. Yet as Rome grew wealthier, these garments became more highly decorated and were made from richer fabrics. Romans became great lovers of jewelry and did not hesitate to display their wealth by wearing numerous jewels. As more and more Romans earned enough money to buy expensive fabrics and adornments, Roman politicians began to limit access to various clothing styles by passing sumptuary laws, which regulated what people could wear and how much money they could spend. Roman clothing also shows the influence of territorial expansion, as the Romans adopted the clothing styles of those they conquered in northern Europe and the fabrics of the Orient. Today we remember Roman clothing through the popular image of the toga, but the Roman clothing tradition offers many other fascinating insights into this amazing ancient society.

FOR MORE INFORMATION

Batterberry, Michael, and Ariane Batterberry. *Fashion: The Mirror of History.* New York: Greenwich House, 1977.

Hart, Avery. *Ancient Rome!: Exploring the Culture, People, and Ideas of This Powerful Empire.* Charlotte, VT: Williamson, 2002.

Hunt, Alan. *Governance of the Consuming Passions: A History of Sumptuary Law.* New York: St. Martin's Press, 1996.

Nardo, Don. *The Ancient Romans.* San Diego, CA: Lucent Books, 2001.

The Roman Empire. http://www.roman-empire.net (accessed on July 11, 2003).

Simpson, Judith. *Ancient Rome.* Alexandria, VA: Time-Life Books, 1997.

Steele, Philip. *Clothes and Crafts in Roman Times.* Milwaukee, WI: Gareth Stevens, 2000.

Symons, David J. *Costume of Ancient Rome.* New York: Chelsea House, 1987.

Roman Clothing

The ancient Romans took the clothing traditions of the past and adapted them into one of the most distinctive costume traditions in all of history. The greatest influences on Roman fashion came from the Etruscans, who developed an advanced society in Italy hundreds of years before the Romans became powerful, and from the Greeks. It was from these two cultures that Romans inherited their love of draped garments. Yet Romans were also influenced greatly by the surrounding peoples they conquered over the years of their expansion. From the Gauls, who lived in present-day France, they inherited a garment something like modern pants, and their trade in the Far East enabled them to use silk and precious stones.

There were two different sides to Roman clothing, however. On the one hand, the Roman clothing tradition was very stable, with the dominant garments staying the same from the time of the founding of the Roman Republic in 509 B.C.E. to the collapse of the Roman Empire in 476 C.E. Yet the materials used to make the garments and the way they were decorated changed a great deal. Garments made from rough wool in the early years were made from rich, imported silk in the later years of the empire (27 B.C.E.–476 C.E.). Strict rules about the kinds of stripes, or clavi, that could be worn on men's tunicas, or shirt, and togas, a long cloak, in the early years gradually disappeared, and men later wore intricately patterned garments.

Romans were also a sharply divided society, with a small number of very wealthy people and masses of poor people. Wealthy Roman men simply did not go outside without a toga draped over a tunica. Respectable women also had an official outfit, consisting of a long dress called a stola, often worn beneath a cloak called a palla. From the lowest classes of society up through royalty, men wore the toga to public ceremonies. It was difficult for the poor people to afford a toga or a stola, yet they had to wear one on certain occasions. Even the poorest Roman citizen, however, was distinguished from slaves or barbarians (the name Romans gave to people from other countries), who were banned from wearing Roman clothes like the toga.

Romans were very careful about the way they dressed. So careful, in fact, that they had a number of rules about who could wear certain items and how certain items should be worn. Romans created some of the first sumptuary laws, which regulated the color and type of clothing that could be worn by members of different social classes. (Sumptuary relates to personal expenditures especially on luxury items.) They also had unwritten rules about such things as the length of a toga or stola and demands for different togas for different social occasions. Wealthy Romans had slaves who helped their masters choose and adjust their clothing to just the right style.

The great philosopher Aristotle, right, teaching his pupil Alexander the Great. Both men wear traditional Roman clothing: Aristotle wears a toga and Alexander wears a tunica.
Reproduced by permission of Getty Images.

Observers have written about how intense the pressure was to wear clothing correctly in ancient Rome.

There is much more of interest about Roman clothing traditions. Because their empire grew so great and took Romans into very different climates, the Romans became the first major society to wear seasonal clothing—that is, clothes for both warm and cold climates. They made warm winter boots and the first known raincoat. The spread of their empire also meant that Roman traditions spread into other countries, particularly throughout Europe and into the British Isles. Variations on ancient Roman costume can still be seen in the vestments, or priestly clothing, worn by members of the Roman Catholic Church.

Most of what we know about Roman clothing comes from evidence left by the wealthiest Romans. The many statues and paintings that have survived, and the various writings from the time, all discuss the clothing styles of those Romans who were very well off. It is likely that poorer Romans wore similar garments, though of much lower quality, but it may be that there were other clothing items that have simply been lost to history.

FOR MORE INFORMATION

Batterberry, Michael, and Ariane Batterberry. *Fashion: The Mirror of History.* New York: Greenwich House, 1977.

Cosgrave, Bronwyn. *The Complete History of Costume and Fashion: From Ancient Egypt to the Present Day.* New York: Checkmark Books, 2000.

Houston, Mary G. *Ancient Greek, Roman, and Byzantine Costume and Decoration.* 2nd ed. New York: Barnes and Noble, 1947.

Sebesta, Judith Lynn, and Larissa Bonfante, eds. *The World of Roman Costume.* Madison, WI: University of Wisconsin Press, 1994.

Steele, Philip. *Clothes and Crafts in Roman Times.* Milwaukee, WI: Gareth Stevens, 2000.

Symons, David J. *Costume of Ancient Rome.* New York: Chelsea House, 1987.

Yates, James. "Solea." *Smith's Dictionary: Articles on Clothing and Adornment.* http://www.ukans.edu/history/index/europe/ancient_rome/E/Roman/Texts/secondary/SMIGRA%2A/Clothing/home%2A.html (accessed on July 24, 2003).

Braccae

Early Romans did not wear pants. Both men and women wore beautiful, draped garments such as the toga or the stola, a long gown that hung nearly to the feet. Leg coverings were seen as crude items, worn by the barbarians who lived beyond the borders of Roman civilization or as the leg protection of the very poor. Yet as the soldiers of the Roman Empire (27 B.C.E.–476 C.E.) began to venture further to distant lands, they began to understand why the peoples of Gaul, present-day France, and Britain wore long pants known as braccae. Simply put, these barbarian garments were needed to keep warm. Other cultures, such as those in Persia, modern-day Iran, and the Middle East, wore pants to protect the legs.

One of two pairs of trousers that the Romans borrowed from conquered peoples—the other were called feminalia—braccae were crude woolen trousers that were secured at the waist with a leather tie and often tied at the ankles as well. The word "braccae" is believed to be the root of the modern word for breeches. Unlike the feminalia, braccae were loose fitting. Those that were modeled after trousers from the warmer Middle East may have been made of cotton or silk. Braccae never came into common use in Rome, the capital of the empire, and some emperors forbade them to be worn in the city. In fact, they seemed so strange and foreign that one of the ways that Roman sculptors and painters identified foreigners was to depict them wearing braccae.

FOR MORE INFORMATION

Yates, James. "Bracae." *Smith's Dictionary: Articles on Clothing and Adornment.* http://www.ukans.edu/history/index/europe/ancient_rome/ E/Roman/Texts/secondary/SMIGRA*/Bracae.html (accessed on July 24, 2003).

[*See also* **Volume 1, Ancient Rome: Feminalia**]

Casula

The casula was a versatile outer garment worn in Rome from about 200 B.C.E. and, in modified forms, is still in use throughout the world today. The casula, which means "little house," was a large rectangular or oval piece of fabric, usually made of wool, into the center of which was cut a hole for the head. This poncho-like garment slipped over the head and protected the user from bad weather, what some may consider an early version of the raincoat. It was often made of a dark color and extended to about the knee.

The casula was actually an adaptation of an older garment, called a paenula. The paenula was a casula with a pointed hood. The casula was itself adopted for use in the Roman Catholic Church as one of the vestments, or ceremonial robes, of the priest. Roman Catholics refer to the garment as the chasuble. Chasubles used by Roman Catholic priests can be very ornate, with colorful patterns and rich embroidery. They are still used to this day.

FOR MORE INFORMATION

Bigelow, Marybelle S. *Fashion in History: Apparel in the Western World.* Minneapolis, MN: Burgess Publishing, 1970.

Payne, Blanche, Geitel Winakor, and Jane Farrell-Beck. *The History of Costume.* 2nd ed. New York: HarperCollins, 1992.

Dalmatica

The dalmatica was a Roman variation of one of the most common garments, the tunica, or shirt. Late in the Roman Empire (27 B.C.E.–476 C.E.) variations on the tunic grew more fanciful and elaborate. One such variation was the dalmatica. At first it had long sleeves and a bell-shaped hem that could reach from the knees to as low as the floor. As time went on, however, the forms of the dalmatica grew more elaborate. Clavi, or stripes, often graced both sides of the garment, and the mode of cutting the sleeves could be narrow at the wrist and broad at the shoulder, or vice versa. Over time the dalmatica became increasingly long and flowing, and it was often worn over a tunica, for men, or in place of the stola, or dress, for women. In this longer form it was adapted as one of the many ecclesiastical or church-related garments worn by clergy in the Roman Catholic Church. The dalmatica also became one of the most common garments of the Byzantine Empire (476–1453 C.E.), which emerged after the collapse of the Roman Empire as the dominant society in the Mediterranean region.

FOR MORE INFORMATION

Payne, Blanche, Geitel Winakor, and Jane Farrell-Beck. *The History of Costume.* 2nd ed. New York: HarperCollins, 1992.

Symons, David J. *Costume of Ancient Rome.* New York: Chelsea House, 1987.

[*See also* **Volume 1, Ancient Rome: Tunica; Volume 2, Byzantine Empire: Dalmatica**]

Etruscan Dress

Before the Romans developed their long-lasting rule on the Italian peninsula, several other groups of people organized towns and farms into small-scale societies. Yet even the most notable and longest lasting of these pre-Roman societies, known as the Etruscans, remains somewhat of a mystery to historians. This is what we know: sometime before 1000 B.C.E. people began to move to the central part of present-day Italy from areas north and east; around 800 B.C.E. more people arrived in the area from Asia Minor, in present-day Turkey. These people, known now as Etruscans, brought with them traditions and costumes from ancient Greek, Mesopotamian (centered in present-day Turkey), and Asian cultures, and they developed a thriving culture of their own. Modeled on the Greek system of loosely linked city-states, the Etruscan culture thrived for several hundred years. Beginning in about 400 B.C.E., however, they came under frequent attack from territories to the north and south. They were brought under Roman rule in 250 B.C.E., and by 80 B.C.E. their culture had been virtually destroyed.

Historians have long thought of the Etruscans as mysterious because they left so few written records. We don't know how they built their society or why it fell apart. We don't know much about the ways that they lived and especially about how the poorer people lived. But we do know quite a bit about the way they dressed, wore their hair, and ornamented themselves. The evidence that survived concerning the Etruscans—paintings, sculpture, and pottery, most of it recovered from burial tombs of the wealthy—indicates that the Etruscans had well-developed costume traditions that combined influences from Greece and Asia. Their costumes had a great influence on the Romans who came to dominate Italy, and the rest of the region, in later years.

Wealthier Etruscans dressed very well indeed. Their clothes were made of fine wool, cotton, and linen, they were often very colorful, and they were based on Greek models. Women, for example, typically wore a gown called a chiton under a shawl called a himation. Both of these garments would have been dyed in bright colors, and evidence indicates that Etruscan women loved to wear

Men wearing Etruscan dress, including tebennas, or long cloaks, with clavi, or stripes.
Reproduced by permission of ©
Archivo Iconografico, S.A./CORBIS.

elaborately patterned garments. Men wore a loin skirt that covered their genitals and often wore a Greek-style tunic. The lacerna, a short woolen cloak, was also very common. By the middle of the sixth century B.C.E. a distinctive garment called a tebenna became the most common male garment. Similar to the Greek chlamys, the tebenna was a long cloak that was draped over the left shoulder and then wrapped around the torso under the right arm. It was often decorated with clavi, stripes of color that indicated the wearer's status or rank in society. The tebenna is thought to be the model for the Roman toga, and Romans also adopted the use of clavi.

One of the highlights of Etruscan costume was its striking jewelry. The Etruscans developed a gold-working technique known as granulation, which involved soldering tiny grains of gold on a smooth background to create a glittering effect. Etruscans wore bracelets, necklaces, earrings, clasps and pins, and other types of jewelry. They also wore makeup and complicated, braided hairstyles. Early Etruscan men wore beards, though later a clean-shaven face became the norm.

Many of the costume traditions of the Etruscans were lost to history, but many others lived on in the traditions of the Romans.

FOR MORE INFORMATION

Bonfante, Larissa. *Etruscan Dress.* Baltimore, MD: Johns Hopkins University Press, 1975.

Cosgrave, Bronwyn. *The Complete History of Costume and Fashion: From Ancient Egypt to the Present Day.* New York: Checkmark Books, 2000.

The Mysterious Etruscans. http://www.mysteriousetruscans.com/index.html (accessed on July 24, 2003).

Feminalia

Feminalia were snugly fitting knee-length pants, or breeches. Though the name might suggest that they were worn by women, in fact they were worn most often by men. They were called feminalia because the pants covered the length of the thighbone, or femur.

During the Roman Republic (509–27 B.C.E.) men had generally avoided wearing trousers or pants of any kind, considering it a barbaric costume. They had good reason for this idea, for the people they saw wearing clothing on their legs were the barbarians who lived on the outskirts of the areas controlled by Rome, especially the loosely organized Gauls who lived in the colder north, in present-day France. During the Roman Empire (27 B.C.E.–476 C.E.), however, Roman soldiers ventured further and further north in pursuit of conquest. Eventually they made their way to Britain, where many men wore pants to protect themselves from the cold. Soon, Roman soldiers, especially horsemen, adopted the short, close-fitting pants of the barbarians, and they returned home with them.

Feminalia never became as popular as the main men's garments, the toga and the tunica, or shirt, but they did become acceptable wear for work or for travel to colder climates. Mounted soldiers, called cavalry, usually wore leather feminalia, similar to the chaps worn by cowboys in the western United States in the nineteenth century. Civilians wore feminalia made from a variety of materials, including wool and cotton. The most famous Roman to wear feminalia was the emperor Augustus Caesar (63 B.C.E.–14 C.E.), who wore them through the winter to protect his sometimes fragile health.

The Roman emperor Nero wearing tight pants called feminalia under his tunic. Feminalia were worn for warmth by Roman soldiers, horsemen, and even emperors. *Reproduced by permission of © Gianni Dagli Orti/CORBIS.*

FOR MORE INFORMATION

Bigelow, Marybelle S. *Fashion in History: Apparel in the Western World.* Minneapolis, MN: Burgess Publishing, 1970.

Payne, Blanche, Geitel Winakor, and Jane Farrell-Beck. *The History of Costume.* 2nd ed. New York: HarperCollins, 1992.

Symons, David J. *Costume of Ancient Rome.* New York: Chelsea House, 1987.

[*See also* **Volume 1, Ancient Rome: Braccae**]

⋮ Palla

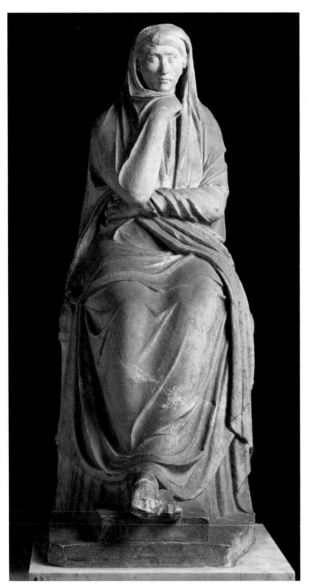

A woman wrapped in a palla. The palla was used as a blanket, a bathrobe, a carpet, or, most commonly, a shawl. *Reproduced by permission of © Araldo de Luca/CORBIS.*

Along with the stola, the palla was the most common piece of clothing worn by women in ancient Rome. It was a very simple garment, yet its simplicity allowed it to be used in a great many ways. The basic palla was a large, rectangular piece of woolen cloth. It was worn wrapped around the body, either over a tunica, or shirt, or a toga if the wearer was unmarried, or over a stola, a long gown, if the wearer was married. Despite its apparent simplicity, the palla has a rich history that stretches back into ancient Greece, and it was adapted into a variety of forms and uses.

As with many of the Roman clothing styles, the palla was an adaptation of a Greek garment. The himation, a large rectangular woolen cloth draped around the body, was worn by both men and women in Greece beginning in the sixth century B.C.E. The garment was soon adopted by the early Romans. For men, the garment was called a pallium, for women a palla. In both Greece and Rome the palla or pallium was put to a variety of uses. It could be used as a blanket at night, thrown on the ground for use as a carpet, wrapped around the body after a bath, strung up to use as a sail on a boat, or draped on a horse for display. All of these uses and more were recorded in ancient Greece and Rome.

Midway through the Roman Republic (509–27 B.C.E.) the pallium went out of use as a garment for men, replaced by the toga, which became the standard male garment. (The pallium remained in use as the characteristic garment of scholars and philosophers, however.) Yet the palla remained an important garment for women, and it was woven and decorated in a variety of fabrics and patterns. Wool was the most common fabric used to make the palla. Types of wool ranged from plain, coarse wool to varieties that had been pounded or washed in ways that increased their softness or changed their texture. Pallas were also made of linen, cotton, and silk, though the latter were worn only by the wealthiest women, for silk had to be imported from the Far East.

Pallas could be of a single, simple color like white, brown, or green, but many women chose to wear much more decorative pallas. Vibrant colors were achieved through the use of exotic dyes, and some weavers excelled at creating intricate patterns similar to plaids. There were many ways of wearing the palla, but the most common was to hang one end of the palla over the front of the left shoulder, then wrap the palla behind the back, under the right arm, and either across the left forearm or over the left shoulder. Other methods might involve tying the palla around the hips, or draping it across the shoulders. Pins or clasps might be used to secure it in place. The palla could also be draped over the head, thus obeying a custom that said well-bred women should keep their head covered in public.

The palla could be used to suit almost any purpose. This is why the palla, or something much like it, has been used by humans in all manners of cultures across human history. Variations on the palla survive today as the shawls and wraps worn by women in Western society.

FOR MORE INFORMATION

Contini, Mila. *Fashion: From Ancient Egypt to the Present Day.* Edited by James Laver. New York: Odyssey Press, 1965.

Symons, David J. *Costume of Ancient Rome.* New York: Chelsea House, 1987.

Yates, James. "Pallium." *Smith's Dictionary: Articles on Clothing and Adornment.* http://www.ukans.edu/history/index/europe/ancient_rome/E/Roman/Texts/secondary/SMIGRA*/Pallium.html (accessed on July 24, 2003).

[*See also* Volume 1, Ancient Greece: Himation; Volume 1, Ancient Rome: Stola]

Stola

The stola was the staple garment of the married woman in ancient Rome. It was a long gown, generally sleeveless, that hung nearly to the feet. The stola was generally worn over a tunica intima, a light inner shirt. It was often fastened at the shoulders by small clasps called fibulae. The stola was typically worn with two belts: one fastened just below the breasts, creating blousy folds, and another wider belt fastened around the waist. The stola could have several forms of decoration. A stola worn by a wealthier woman might have a limbus, a separate piece of fabric with many folds that was sewn into the hem, making it appear that another gown was worn beneath. Simpler stolas had a band of color or a pattern at the hem and many stolas had a band of color near the neckline. Stolas appeared to have been made in a variety of colors, from bleached white to red, yellow, and blue. Stolas were generally made of wool or cotton, but wealthy women might wear a stola made of silk.

As well as being a functional piece of clothing, the stola served an important social function. In ancient Rome the position that people occupied in society was very important, and clothes were used as symbols of social position or status. The stola was a sign that the woman wearing it was married. Single women or divorced women were forbidden from wearing the stola.

Like most of women's clothing in ancient Rome, the stola changed very little over time. Statues dating from early in the Roman Republic (509–27 B.C.E.) to late in the Roman Empire (27 B.C.E.–476 C.E.) all show women garbed in a similar, traditional stola, usually accompanied by the other staple women's garment, the palla, a large wrap.

FOR MORE INFORMATION

Cosgrave, Bronwyn. *The Complete History of Costume and Fashion: From Ancient Egypt to the Present Day.* New York: Checkmark Books, 2000.

Robinson, Scott R. "Roman." *Costume History.* http://www.cwu.edu/robinsos/ppages/resources/Costume_History/roman.htm (accessed on July 24, 2003).

Symons, David J. *Costume of Ancient Rome.* New York: Chelsea House, 1987.

[*See also* **Volume 1, Ancient Rome: Palla; Volume 1, Ancient Rome: Tunica**]

Subligaculum

A form of underwear worn by both men and women in ancient Rome, the subligaculum was one of the most basic garments. It was very similar to the perizoma, a tight-fitting pair of shirt pants, worn by the Etruscans, a pre-Roman society that inhabited the central part of present-day Italy, and the Etruscans in turn appear to have adapted the garment from examples worn by ancient Greeks and Egyptians. A basic loincloth, the main purpose of the subligaculum was to cover the genitals. Like other loin coverings worn in ancient times, the subligaculum came in a number of forms. At its simplest, it might consist of a belt with a piece of fabric stretching from front to back between the legs. More substantial subligaculums might cover all of the buttocks and tie at the sides.

Most people wore the subligaculum under other garments. For example, men wore the garment under the tunica (shirt) or the toga, and women wore it under the stola, a long gown. But others wore the subligaculum alone. Common workers often labored wearing only a subligaculum, and Roman gladiators, warriors who fought for entertainment in Rome, usually fought wearing just a subligaculum.

Our knowledge of Roman costume generally comes from the many statues, bas-reliefs, wall carvings, and paintings that have been recovered by archeologists, scientists who study the physical remains of past cultures. Yet these statues and paintings don't reveal what was worn beneath the outer garments. Historians aren't sure what Romans were wearing underneath their flowing togas and stolas, but their best guess is that it was a subligaculum.

FOR MORE INFORMATION

Symons, David J. *Costume of Ancient Rome.* New York: Chelsea House, 1987.

Toga

If you had to choose one garment to represent the costume traditions of ancient Rome, that garment would be the toga. It can be seen on statues and paintings of Roman men from the earliest founding of the city of Rome in 753 B.C.E. until the collapse of the Roman Empire in 476 C.E. During the years of the Roman Republic (509–27 B.C.E.), Romans were often called gens togata, or people of the toga. The toga remains familiar to people today because it has been so widely used in Hollywood films, from early epics such as *Ben-Hur* (1959) to rowdy comedies such as *Animal House* (1978), which made the toga party a popular college ritual. The toga is undoubtedly the best-known garment from the ancient world.

A man wearing a pink toga, one of the most familiar garments of the Romans. *Reproduced by permission of © Gianni Dagli Orti/CORBIS.*

The toga has its roots in garments worn by the Etruscans and the Greeks. The Greeks had worn a lengthy cloak called the himation, and the Etruscans, early inhabitants of the Italian peninsula, had adapted this into their tebenna. But the true toga was a Roman invention. In the early days of the republic, when Roman society first became quite organized and identifiable, the toga was a rather small elongated oval of woolen fabric and was easily worn over the top of the tunica, or shirt. Though there were many different ways of wearing the toga, the most common way involved holding the toga behind the back and draping one end of the toga forward across the left shoulder, so that the end hung between the legs. The remainder of the toga was crossed under, and sometimes around, the right arm, across the chest, and then back over the left shoulder. It was possible to lift a portion of the toga over the back of the head, forming a type of hood.

During the early republic, the toga was practically required for any but the lowest of Roman workers. It was always worn by more notable citizens and was forbidden to slaves and foreigners. Though women wore togas at first, they soon abandoned the garment for the palla, a type of cloak.

Toga styles

Though the basic shape of all togas was roughly the same, there were important variations in color and decoration that offered clues as to the wearer's place in society. The common toga was known simply as the toga virilis, and it was left in the natural color of wool. When campaigning for public office, candidates wore a toga candida, which was bleached to a bright white. Though the toga was typically worn over a tunica, candidates sometimes went bare chested beneath the toga candida to show off their battle scars. The toga picta, favored by later emperors, was a ceremonial toga, covered in ornate embroidery that was first worn by victorious generals in public ceremonies. Though most togas were light in color, the toga pulla, which was worn by mourners, was a dark shade, such as black, dark brown, or gray. Children might wear a toga praetexta, which had a broad purple border; the toga praetexta was also worn by magistrates, local judges. It was modeled closely after an Etruscan tebenna. Finally, priests wore a toga trabea that had red stripes and a purple border. The toga trabea worn by other religious figures had slightly different coloring. In addition, different types of togas might have clavi, which are stripes that run the length of the garment.

The difficulties of the toga

Roman costume in general grew more complicated over time, and the toga was no exception. First, the toga grew greatly in size. From an easy to wear cloak, the toga grew to a size of about eighteen feet long by about eleven feet wide. Draping the toga about the body became a difficult chore. While wealthy Romans were helped with their wrapping by servants or slaves, the common Roman person had to struggle with it on his own. Not wearing a toga wasn't an option. All Roman citizens were required to wear the toga at public ceremonies, and going without the toga in public was considered disrespectable.

The size of the toga caused other problems as well. As the togas grew larger, they got heavy and hot. The wearer's left arm was usually enclosed in fabric, and the right arm was usually used to hold the toga in place. It was difficult to do anything while wearing a toga, especially anything active. Finally, distinctions about how long togas were supposed to be, and how the front folds were supposed to drape, became very important but required that the wearer constantly worry whether their toga style was in fashion. A Roman writer and an observer of Roman costumes named Tertullian (c. 155–c. 220 C.E.), quoted in Michael and Ariane Batterberry's *Fashion: The Mirror of History,* said of the toga: "It is not a garment, but a burden."

Eventually, sometime after about 200 C.E., the toga was discarded as a common garment. Common people simply didn't have the time or the money to keep their togas in proper condition for public wear, and others grew tired of trying to accomplish their daily tasks while wearing the cumbersome cloak. The toga was still worn for ceremonial occasions, but most Romans wore the simpler tunica, sometimes with a range of other, simpler outer garments.

FOR MORE INFORMATION

Batterberry, Michael, and Ariane Batterberry. *Fashion: The Mirror of History.* New York: Greenwich House, 1977.

Cosgrave, Bronwyn. *The Complete History of Costume and Fashion: From Ancient Egypt to the Present Day.* New York: Checkmark Books, 2000.

Houston, Mary G. *Ancient Greek, Roman, and Byzantine Costume and Decoration.* 2nd ed. New York: Barnes and Noble, 1947.

Smith, William. "Toga." *Smith's Dictionary: Articles on Clothing and Adornment.* http://www.ukans.edu/history/index/europe/ancient_rome/E/Roman/Texts/secondary/SMIGRA*/Toga.html (accessed on July 24, 2003).

Symons, David J. *Costume of Ancient Rome.* New York: Chelsea House, 1987.

[*See also* **Volume 1, Ancient Greece: Himation; Volume 1, Ancient Rome: Etruscan Dress; Volume 1, Ancient Rome: Tunica**]

Tunica

Through the course of Roman history, from the early years of ancient Rome in 753 B.C.E. to the fall of the Roman Empire in

476 C.E., there were two garments that were essential to the male wardrobe: the tunica and the toga. Adapted from the Greek chiton, the tunica, a type of shirt, was the simplest of garments. It was made from two rectangular pieces of fabric, one set on top of the other. It was sewn together at the sides and the top, with holes left for the head and the arms. Tunicas could also have sleeves, ranging from very short in the early republic to full length later in the empire. From these simple foundations, the Romans made the tunica into a garment capable of sending complex messages about taste, social status, and power.

Though the tunica (the Latin word for tunic) was worn by all men in ancient Rome, the type of fabric it was made of and the way it was worn marked important social differences. At the bottom of the social scale, men wore a simple tunica made of undyed, rough wool. They might wear a simple belt around the tunica or leave it unbelted. Some working men wore a tunic that fastened over only one shoulder, called an exomis. Members of the middle classes and wealthier citizens would not have worn a tunica outdoors without a toga, a long cloak; to do so was to be considered "nudus," which meant either nude or underdressed. Tunicas of middle- and upper-class citizens were made of softer wool, and later of linen and cotton. In cooler seasons, wealthier men often wore two tunicas, a tunica interior and a tunica exterior. The emperor Augustus Caesar (63 B.C.E.–14 C.E.) was said to have worn four tunicas during cold weather. Wealthy men paid a great deal of attention to how their tunicas were belted. They used either a narrow belt or a wider girdle, which might have pockets to hold personal belongings. They pulled the tunica fabric up above the belt to get the tunica to just the right length.

Tunica patterns and styles also changed a great deal over the thousand years of Roman history. In early Rome, for example, long sleeves were considered unmanly and tunics were cut above the knee. By the later empire, after the second century C.E., long sleeves were common and tunicas extended almost to the feet. One of the primary forms of decorating a tunica was the use of clavi, dyed stripes that ran vertically down the tunica from each shoulder. The width and color of clavi indicated a person's social position. The tunica angusti clavi, which was worn by knights and judges, had narrow purple stripes. The tunica laticlavia, worn by senators, had wide purple stripes. A very special tunica called a tunica palmate was worn by victorious generals and emperors. It was made of purple silk, embroidered with gold thread, and worn with a special toga.

All Roman fashions became more elaborate and decorative over the course of the Roman Empire (27 B.C.E.–476 C.E.) and the tunica was no exception. Tunicas were worn in several varieties. The colobium, like early tunicas, had short sleeves and came to the knee, but it was much baggier. The dalmatica, which was worn by women as well as men, had long, baggy sleeves and often reached to the floor. Increasingly, Romans wore their tunicas without a belt or girdle, so that the fabric billowed about the body. For many women the longer, blousy tunica took the place of the stola, the traditional female garment. During the empire, tunicas also became more decorative. Tunicas with clavi were worn by people of all classes, and the stripes became more elaborate, with rich colors and patterns. Tunicas might also have striped bands on the sleeves and patterned panels.

Though tunicas are generally thought of as a male garment, they were also worn by poorer women and by children of all classes. The tunicas worn by children mirrored the styles of their parents. The tunica was truly an all-purpose garment, and it survives in its basic form in many modern clothes, including the T-shirt.

FOR MORE INFORMATION

Cosgrave, Bronwyn. *The Complete History of Costume and Fashion: From Ancient Egypt to the Present Day.* New York: Checkmark Books, 2000.

Symons, David J. *Costume of Ancient Rome.* New York: Chelsea House, 1987.

Yates, James. "Tunica." *Smith's Dictionary: Articles on Clothing and Adornment.* http://www.ukans.edu/history/index/europe/ancient_rome/E/Roman/Texts/secondary/SMIGRA*/Tunica.html (accessed on July 24, 2003).

[*See also* **Volume 1, Ancient Rome: Dalmatica; Volume 1, Ancient Rome: Stola; Volume 1, Ancient Rome: Toga**]

Roman Headwear

The costume traditions of the ancient Romans were, in general, fairly simple. Romans did not tend to wear hats or decorative headdresses throughout the long history of their civilization, which lasted from the founding of the city of Rome in 753 B.C.E. to the fall of the Roman Empire in 476 C.E. But this does not mean that Roman customs and traditions of hair and hairstyling were not important. In fact, Romans had some interesting rituals relating to hair. They believed that washing their hair too frequently would disturb the spirits that watched over them. Yet they also believed that it was very important to wash their hair on August 13 as a celebration of the birthday of Diana, the goddess of the hunt. Sailors believed that it was back luck to cut their hair aboard ship—except during a storm.

Men's hairstyles

Men's hairstyles in ancient Rome were very simple. Prior to the introduction of the razor in Rome in about 300 B.C.E., men tended to wear both their hair and their beards long. After the introduction of the razor, however, short hair, combed forward, became the most common hairstyle for men. This hairstyle, known as the Caesar, remains popular to this day. It was named after the Roman general and statesman Julius Caesar (100–44 B.C.E.). As for beards, they went in and out of style, depending on whether they were favored by the emperor at the time.

Though men typically did not wear hats, they could wear a ceremonial form of headwear known as a corona, or crown. Like many areas of Roman dress, there were strict rules about wearing coronas. For example, a gold crown decorated with the towers of a castle could only be worn by the first soldier to scale the walls of a city under attack. The most honored corona was made from weeds, grass, and

Romans did not usually wear hats throughout their history. Before the introduction of the razor in Rome, in about 300 B.C.E., men tended to wear their hair and beards long. *Reproduced by permission of © Archivo Iconografico, S.A./CORBIS.*

wildflowers collected from a Roman city held siege by an enemy, and it was given to the general who broke the siege. Other ceremonial coronas were worn at civic occasions such as weddings and funerals. The notion that only an emperor wore a laurel wreath is actually a historical myth. Any victorious general could wear a laurel wreath.

Women's hairstyles

In the early years of Roman history, women tended to wear their hair long and very simply. They parted it in the center and gathered it behind the head in a bun or a ponytail. Though women's clothing remained fairly simple, their hairstyles grew more and more complex, especially after the founding of the Roman Empire in 27 B.C.E. With the help of slaves trained especially in hair styling, they curled and braided their hair, piling it on the top and back of their head and sometimes holding it in place with very simple headdresses. Archeologists, scientists who study the physical remains of the past, have discovered a wide array of hair grooming accessories in the tombs of Roman women, including hair curlers, pins, and ribbons.

Both men and women resorted to other means to change their hair. Dyeing the hair was very popular among women, with blonde being a favorite color. Men might also dye their hair. Men and women also wore wigs and hair extensions.

FOR MORE INFORMATION

"Coma." *Smith's Dictionary: Articles on Clothing and Adornment.* http://www.ukans.edu/history/index/europe/ancient_rome/E/Roman/Texts/secondary/SMIGRA*/Coma.html (accessed on July 24, 2003).

"Corona." *Smith's Dictionary: Articles on Clothing and Adornment.* http://www.ukans.edu/history/index/europe/ancient_rome/E/Roman/Texts/secondary/SMIGRA*/Corona.html (accessed on July 24, 2003).

Corson, Richard. *Fashions in Hair: The First Five Thousand Years.* London, England: Peter Owen, 2001.

Cosgrave, Bronwyn. *The Complete History of Costume and Fashion: From Ancient Egypt to the Present Day.* New York: Checkmark Books, 2000.

Symons, David J. *Costume of Ancient Rome.* New York: Chelsea House, 1987.

Trasko, Mary. *Daring Do's: A History of Extraordinary Hair.* New York: Flammarion, 1994.

Beards

When it came to the wearing of facial hair, Roman men went through several shifts in style over the long history of their civilization. From the founding of Rome in 753 B.C.E. until about 300 B.C.E., all men wore long beards and long hair. In a way, they had no choice, for razors hadn't been invented. Then, in about 300 B.C.E., a barber from the island of Sicily introduced the razor and everything changed. For the next several hundred years Roman men followed a simple rule about facial hair: slaves wore beards and free men and citizens did not. It took a vain emperor to change men's beard styles again.

The emperor Hadrian (76–138 C.E.) came to power as a result of his skills as a military general, and he ruled the Roman Empire from 117 to 138 C.E. In order to hide his facial scars, Hadrian wore a beard and curly hair. (In fact, it is likely that he curled both his hair and his beard.) In ancient Rome the emperor held all the power, and men across the empire followed his lead. Thus, beards once again came in style. Slaves, on the other hand, began to shave. When the emperor Constantine (c. 285–337 C.E.) came into power in 306 C.E., he brought a clean-shaven face back into fashion again.

When beards were in fashion, men took great care of them. They visited barbers to have their beards clipped, plucked, and curled. Wealthy men kept slaves whose sole duty was to care for their master's hair.

FOR MORE INFORMATION

Batterberry, Michael, and Ariane Batterberry. *Fashion: The Mirror of History.* New York: Greenwich House, 1977.

Cosgrave, Bronwyn. *The Complete History of Costume and Fashion: From Ancient Egypt to the Present Day.* New York: Checkmark Books, 2000.

Symons, David J. *Costume of Ancient Rome.* New York: Chelsea House, 1987.

Braids and Curls

One thing is made very clear by the statues, coins, and paintings that provide our evidence about the hairstyles worn in ancient Rome: women changed their hairstyles very often. Though there is no one typical Roman hairstyle, it is obvious that Roman women often curled and braided their hair.

Perhaps to make up for the simplicity of their wardrobe, including the fact that Romans didn't wear hats, Roman women wore elaborate hairstyles. From the early years of the Roman Republic (509–27 B.C.E.), women began to coil their long hair into a crown on their head. They might braid the hair first and then wrap it into intricate designs. They also used a device called a calamistrum to curl their hair. The calamistrum was a hollow iron tube that was heated. Hair was rolled around it, and when it was removed the hair retained its curly shape. These early hair curlers were very common among wealthy Roman women, and men sometimes had their hair curled as well.

During the Roman Empire (27 B.C.E.–476 C.E.), when Roman civilization was at its height of power, women took their braided and curled hairstyles to extremes. They were careful never to appear in public without carefully tended hair, and they kept slaves, known as ornatrices, who were specially trained in hair styling.

Carving of a Roman man with long braids. Both men and women wore braids and curls in their hair. *Reproduced by permission of © Araldo de Luca/CORBIS.*

FOR MORE INFORMATION

Batterberry, Michael, and Ariane Batterberry. *Fashion: The Mirror of History.* New York: Greenwich House, 1977.

Cosgrave, Bronwyn. *The Complete History of Costume and Fashion: From Ancient Egypt to the Present Day.* New York: Checkmark Books, 2000.

Yates, James. "Calamistrum." *Smith's Dictionary: Articles on Clothing and Adornment.* http://www.ukans.edu/history/index/europe/ancient_rome/E/Roman/Texts/secondary/SMIGRA*/Calamistrum.html (accessed on July 24, 2003).

Hair Coloring

By the time of the Roman Empire (27 B.C.E.–476 C.E.), both men and women had largely given up the customs of simplicity and frugality that characterized early Rome. One of the most popular ways for people to ornament themselves was through hair dyes. The many traders and slaves that came to Rome and other Roman cities as a result of the empire's great expansion exposed the Romans to a wide variety of hair colors.

The most popular hair coloring in ancient Rome was blond, which was associated with the exotic and foreign appearance of people from Gaul, present-day France, and Germany. Roman prostitutes were required by law to dye their hair blond in order to set themselves apart, but many Roman women and men followed suit. The other most popular hair colors were red and black. The most striking hair coloring effects of all could only be afforded by the very wealthiest Romans; some of them powdered their hair with gold dust. The emperor Commodus (161–192 C.E.), who ruled from 180 to 192 C.E., was especially famous for powdering his snow-white hair with gold.

Romans used a variety of methods and ingredients for dyeing their hair. Some used henna, a plant-based reddish brown dye, and others used berries, vinegar, or crushed nutshells. Perhaps the strangest hair dye was a preparation used to turn the hair black that was made from leeches mixed with vinegar. Women would allow this awful mixture to ferment; after two months they would apply it to their hair and sit in the sun to allow it to bake in. People have continued to color their hair throughout history, but thankfully dyeing techniques have become a bit more pleasant.

FOR MORE INFORMATION

Batterberry, Michael, and Ariane Batterberry. *Fashion: The Mirror of History.* New York: Greenwich House, 1977.

"Coma." *Smith's Dictionary: Articles on Clothing and Adornment.* http://www.ukans.edu/history/index/europe/ancient_rome/E/Roman/Texts/secondary/SMIGRA*/Coma.html (accessed on July 24, 2003).

Cosgrave, Bronwyn. *The Complete History of Costume and Fashion: From Ancient Egypt to the Present Day.* New York: Checkmark Books, 2000.

[*See also* **Volume 3, Sixteenth Century: Hair Coloring; Volume 5, 1946–60: Hair Coloring**]

Wigs

During the Roman Empire (27 B.C.E.–476 C.E.) wealthy members of Roman society developed a rich and fashionable lifestyle, which included much attention to appearance and ornamentation. Both women and men used any means available to improve their looks and decorate their bodies. Cosmetics and luxurious costumes were used, and elaborate hairstyles came into fashion for women. Baldness in men was viewed as an ugly defect. Both women and men made frequent use of wigs to hide any shortage of hair.

The citizens of the vigorous Roman Republic, which thrived between 509 and 27 B.C.E., had valued simple styles in hair and clothing. Even the wealthy styled their hair plainly, though they may have curled it with hot irons. By the time of the Roman Empire (27 B.C.E.–476 C.E.), which saw the Roman people grow in wealth and power, styles had changed, and luxury and excess were in fashion for those who could afford them. Though hairstyles for men remained short and simple, most who suffered hair loss were unwilling to have their lack of hair exposed. Julius Caesar, the famous general and leader of Rome who lived from 100 to 44 B.C.E., frequently wore a laurel wreath to hide his baldness. Other wealthy Romans glued hairpieces onto their scalps for the same reason.

During the Roman Empire, Roman women began to wear more and more elaborate hairstyles, with masses of corkscrew curls piled high on the fronts of their heads. The Empress Messalina, who lived from 22 to 48 C.E. and was married to Emperor Claudius I (10 B.C.E.–54 C.E.), became famous for the complicated and showy hairstyles she wore. Soon other noble women copied the empress. Women who did not have enough hair to achieve the ornate styles wore wigs or added extra false hair to their own. It became especially popular to use blond or red hair that was bought or taken from slaves and prisoners of war from more northern countries like Gaul (present-day France) and Germany. Blond hair had once been associated only with Roman prostitutes, but once the empress began to wear it, the shame attached to blond hair disappeared. Eventually light-colored northern hair became so popular that a lively trade developed, and red and golden hair became a sort of currency.

The dramatic hairstyles of wealthy Roman women changed so frequently that even sculptures began to have a sort of wig. Many notable women who had their portraits carved in marble began to ask that the hair be carved as a separate piece, so that the hair on the sculpture could be changed to keep up with the current fashion.

FOR MORE INFORMATION

Batterberry, Michael, and Ariane Batterberry. *Fashion: The Mirror of History.* New York: Greenwich House, 1977.

Black, J. Anderson, and Madge Garland. Updated and revised by Frances Kennett. *A History of Fashion.* New York: William Morrow, 1980.

Roman Body Decorations

Roman attitudes toward the grooming and decoration of their bodies changed dramatically over the course of the long history of their civilization. From the serious and simple habits of the eighth-century-B.C.E. founders of the city of Rome, Romans became increasingly concerned with bathing, jewelry, and makeup. By the time of the Roman Empire (27 B.C.E.–476 C.E.), bathing had become an elaborate public ritual, wealthy Romans imported precious jewels from throughout their vast empire, and women wore complicated cosmetics.

The early inhabitants of Rome dressed and decorated themselves rather simply. They might bathe their arms and legs daily, but they only took a full bath about once a week. As Roman wealth and luxury grew, however, more and more Romans began to attend public baths. Public baths were civic gathering places, perhaps like a modern gym or health club, dedicated to bathing and exercise. In the larger towns these public baths were very elaborate. They had sauna rooms and heated and chilled pools. Romans developed complex rituals about their baths; they might move through four baths of different temperatures before exercising. Men and women bathed separately: women typically bathed every morning, while men bathed in the late afternoon. All citizens in a town could attend the public baths for a small fee, but the wealthiest Roman citizens had richly decorated private baths.

For men daily bathing was the primary form of body care, and they used few ornaments to decorate themselves, other than perhaps a signet ring, often a gold ring with a decorative stone at its center. Roman women, however, developed a great love of makeup and jewelry. Following their baths, women might use a variety of different forms of skin cream, perfumed oils, and makeup. Their makeup was made from foul-smelling ingredients such as

An intricately designed gold Roman necklace. As the Roman Empire began to prosper, jewelry became more ornate and **expensive.** *Reproduced by permission of © David Lees/ CORBIS.*

milk and animal fat, and perhaps they wore strong perfumes to mask the odor. Roman women also applied beauty spots, or colored patches, to their faces.

The Romans inherited from their Etruscan neighbors (in present-day central Italy) a great love of jewelry, and as their society grew richer over time the wealthiest Romans were able to purchase and wear many different kinds of jewelry. Perhaps the most favored kind of jewelry was pearls. The simple bulla, a kind of necklace, was worn by Romans of all classes, however.

FOR MORE INFORMATION

Batterberry, Michael, and Ariane Batterberry. *Fashion: The Mirror of History.* New York: Greenwich House, 1977.

Cosgrave, Bronwyn. *The Complete History of Costume and Fashion: From Ancient Egypt to the Present Day.* New York: Checkmark Books, 2000.

Rich, Anthony. "Balneae." *Smith's Dictionary: Articles on Clothing and Adornment.* http://www.ukans.edu/history/index/europe/ancient_rome/ E/Roman/Texts/secondary/SMIGRA*/Balneae.html (accessed on July 24, 2003).

Bulla

Both rich and poor Roman parents hung a bulla around their newborn child's neck to protect him or her from misfortune or injury. A bulla could be as simple as a knotted string of cheap leather or as elaborate as a finely made chain necklace holding a golden locket containing a charm thought to have protective qualities. Girls wore their bullas until their wedding day and boys wore theirs until they became citizens (full members of society) at age sixteen. Some men, such as generals, would wear their bullas at ceremonies to protect them from the jealousy of others. Although bullae (plural of bulla) had spiritual and legal significance, during Roman times, the Etruscans, from modern-day central Italy, wore embossed bullae in groups of three as purely decorative ornaments for necklaces and bracelets or, for men, as symbols of military victories.

FOR MORE INFORMATION

Payne, Blanche, Geitel Winakor, and Jane Farrell-Beck. *The History of Costume: From Ancient Mesopotamia Through the Twentieth Century.* 2nd ed. New York: HarperCollins, 1992.

Jewelry

Although Roman clothing styles in general are known for their simplicity and lack of ornament, the widespread use of jewelry provided Roman women with a rare opportunity for display. (The only form of jewelry worn by men was the signet ring, often a gold ring with a decorative stone at its center.) Fashion historians believe that the Romans inherited their love of jewelry from the Etruscans who lived in Italy before the establishment of the Roman Republic in 509 B.C.E. The Etruscans had a great love of jewelry. They wore bracelets, earrings, and rings. One custom they seemed to have begun was wearing several rings on each hand. They also developed a unique technique for making gold jewelry called granulation. This involved soldering tiny grains of gold on a solid gold background, which made the item sparkle. This gold-working technique was lost for many centuries and was not recovered until the nineteenth century.

Early Roman jewelry was modeled on Greek and Etruscan examples and remained fairly simple. As Roman armies ventured further from Italy in source of conquest, they began to return home with new jewels and precious stones. During the period of the

Roman Empire (27 B.C.E.–476 C.E.), as the empire began to prosper and many people became more affluent, Roman jewelry became much more ornate. Instead of glass and semiprecious stones, jewelry now included opals, emeralds, sapphires, and diamonds. (Diamonds were uncut, however, and were always mounted in rings.) The most precious items used for jewelry were pearls, which arrived from Ceylon (present-day Sri Lanka), off the coast of India.

During the Roman Empire women wore jewelry of all types: earrings, rings for the fingers and toes, bracelets, anklets, and necklaces. Fibulae, or clasps, were used to hold clothing in place and were made in great variety. Contemporary observers took notice of the great wealth of jewelry worn by Roman women. For example, Lollia Paulina (d. 49 C.E.), the wife of the Roman emperor Caligula (12–41 C.E.), had a set of pearls and emeralds that would be worth several million dollars today.

FOR MORE INFORMATION

Batterberry, Michael, and Ariane Batterberry. *Fashion: The Mirror of History.* New York: Greenwich House, 1977.

Cosgrave, Bronwyn. *The Complete History of Costume and Fashion: From Ancient Egypt to the Present Day.* New York: Checkmark Books, 2000.

Symons, David J. *Costume of Ancient Rome.* New York: Chelsea House, 1987.

[*See also* Volume 1, Ancient Greece: Fibulae; Volume 1, Ancient Rome: Signet Ring]

Makeup

Roman philosopher and playwright Plautus (c. 254–184 B.C.E.) once wrote, "A woman without paint is like food without salt." Like the Greeks before them, Roman women, and some men, used a variety of preparations to improve their appearance. The most common form of makeup used was face paint, called fucus, spread all over the face to make it appear white. This white paste might be infused with a red dye to make rouge for the cheeks or the lips, or tinted with soot to darken the brows or the eyelashes. People also coated their bodies in oils, either plain olive oil early in the Roman Republic (509–27 B.C.E.) or fragrant oil later in the Roman Empire (27 B.C.E.–476 C.E.).

The ancient Romans probably needed the fragrant oils, because their makeup was made of ingredients that must have produced a terrible stink. The wife of Emperor Nero, who ruled from 54 to 68 C.E., used a facial mask made from sheep fat, breadcrumbs, and milk. According to historian Bronwyn Cosgrave in *The Complete History of Costume and Fashion: From Ancient Egypt to the Present Day,* "This mixture often produced a sickening odor if it was left to sit for more than a few hours." Other ingredients, however, may have been worse: Roman documents report that some women used a paste made from calf genitals dissolved in sulfur and vinegar, others used a concoction made from crocodile feces, and still others used oils gathered from the sweatiest parts of sheep (today the last ingredient is called lanolin, and it is used it in many skin products). By comparison, the usual facial pastes made of lead, honey, and fat must have smelled quite nice, though the lead in them could cause lead poisoning and possibly lead to death. Makeup wearers in ancient Rome certainly knew the meaning of the saying "Beauty is pain."

FOR MORE INFORMATION

Batterberry, Michael, and Ariane Batterberry. *Fashion: The Mirror of History.* New York: Greenwich House, 1977.

Cosgrave, Bronwyn. *The Complete History of Costume and Fashion: From Ancient Egypt to the Present Day.* New York: Checkmark Books, 2000.

Schmitz, Leonhard. "Unguenta." *Smith's Dictionary: Articles on Clothing and Adornment.* http://www.ukans.edu/history/index/europe/ancient_rome/E/Roman/Texts/secondary/SMIGRA*/Unguenta.html (accessed on July 24, 2003).

[*See also* **Volume 1, Ancient Greece: Makeup**]

Signet Ring

The most important piece of jewelry for men during the Roman Empire (27 B.C.E.–476 C.E.) was a signet ring, also called a seal ring. Signet rings were first made out of iron but later came to be made more commonly of gold, especially for government officials and honored military men. The center of the signet ring held a stone ornament. The stone, engraved with the wearer's initials and sometimes decorated with a picture, such as the head of the Greek hero Hercules, was used to stamp the wearer's signature in sealing wax to authorize important documents. Although no longer used for signatures, signet rings remain popular pieces of jewelry for men in many Western cultures.

FOR MORE INFORMATION

Norris, Herbert. *Costume and Fashion: The Evolution of European Dress Through the Earlier Ages.* London, England: J. M. Dent and Sons, 1924. Reprint, New York: E. P. Dutton, 1931.

Roman Footwear

Along with the inhabitants of India, the ancient Romans were one of the first peoples in recorded history to develop a wide range of footwear. The ancient Mesopotamians (inhabitants of the region centered in present-day Iraq), Egyptians, and Greeks either went barefoot or used simple sandals as their dominant form of footwear. The climate in these regions made such footwear choices reasonable. But the more variable climate on the Italian peninsula, home to the Etruscans and to the Romans, made wearing sandals or going barefoot uncomfortable. These societies developed many different styles of footwear, from light sandals for indoor wear to heavy boots for military use or for travel to colder climates. Leather was the primary material used for making footwear in ancient Rome. The Romans were very skilled at making quality leather from the hides of cows.

Etruscan footwear

The Etruscans, who preceded the Romans in creating a fully developed society on the Italian peninsula from as early as about 800 B.C.E., developed several different forms of footwear. We know little about Etruscan footwear, however, because few records of their culture remain. They are often referred to as the "mysterious" Etruscans. But historians do think that they borrowed footwear styles from the Greeks and from the Far East, perhaps from the societies of India. The available evidence, primarily statues and some wall paintings, as well as Roman histories, indicates that the Etruscans wore light sandals, slippers made of cloth (probably wool), and leather boots that were held closed with leather straps. One form of sandal which had pointy toes that curled upward seemed to be borrowed from eastern Asia. All but this last style can be seen in later Roman shoes.

The shoes of the Romans

The basic types of footwear worn by the Romans changed very little from the formation of the Roman Republic in 509 B.C.E. to the fall of the Roman Empire in 476 C.E. The basic outdoor shoe was known as the calceus. This shoe covered the entire foot and was closed with leather laces, called thongs. Another slightly lighter outdoor shoe was called the crepida. It covered the sides and the back of the foot, and could be made in several different styles. The Romans also wore several styles of boot. The cothurnus, a high ornate boot, was worn by horsemen, hunters, and some authority figures to show their status. It was a high, ornate boot. Another style of boot, adopted by the Romans from the inhabitants of a conquered region known as Gaul, in present-day France, was called the gallicae. It was a rugged boot made for work and for cold weather. Finally, Romans wore several styles of shoes indoors. Most common was the solea, or sandal. A light shoe of leather or woven papyrus leaves, the solea was held to the foot with a simple strap across the top of the foot, or instep. Other indoor shoes included the soccus, a loose leather slipper, and the sandalium, a wooden-soled sandal worn primarily by women.

Roman men wearing a basic Roman sandal. Romans used different footwear styles to indicate the status and power of the wearer. *Reproduced by permission of © Stapleton Collection/CORBIS.*

Though the basic types of footwear remained the same during Roman history, the styles did change over time. Footwear styles before and during the Roman Republic (509–27 B.C.E.) were plain, with little ornament, expressing the simplicity and frugality of the early Romans. With the rise of the Roman Empire after 27 B.C.E., which saw the Roman people grow in wealth and power, footwear styles became more ornate and decorative. Wealthy people especially often wore shoes that had gold trim or ornaments, metal buckles, embroidery, or jewels.

As with other forms of clothing, the Romans used differences in footwear styles to indicate the status and power of the wearer. For example, the senators who made the laws in Roman times wore a special form of calceus that was secured with four black thongs, while emperors wore calcei (plural of calceus) that were secured with red thongs. Slaves, on the other hand, were not allowed to wear calcei at all. They went barefoot. And prisoners were often forced to wear heavy wooden crepidae that made it difficult for them to walk. The actors in Roman dramas also used footwear to symbolize the status of the characters that they played. Comic actors wore light, leather crepidae, while actors in more serious plays, called tragedies, wore cothurni (the plural of cothurnus). Just like today, you could tell a lot about a person in ancient Rome by the kind of shoes they wore.

FOR MORE INFORMATION

Cosgrave, Bronwyn. *The Complete History of Costume and Fashion: From Ancient Egypt to the Present Day.* New York: Checkmark Books, 2000.

The Mysterious Etruscans. http://www.mysterioustuscans.com/index.html (accessed on July 24, 2003).

Symons, David J. *Costume of Ancient Rome.* New York: Chelsea House, 1987.

Calceus

The calceus was the first shoe in history to look like modern dress shoes. A special type of calceus had been worn by Etruscan kings, who ruled parts of the Italian peninsula before the Romans. In common usage beginning in the Roman Republic (509–27 B.C.E.), the calceus had a leather upper secured to a sole that could be made of leather or wood. Calcei (the plural of calceus) were worn outside with the toga, the traditional outer garment worn by Roman citizens. Along with the solea, or sandal, the calceus was the most common form of footwear worn in ancient Rome.

The calceus could take many forms. At its simplest it was a kind of moccasin, made from a single piece of leather that wrapped around the sole of the foot and laced together over the arch. But as

Roman shoemaking skills grew more advanced so did the calceus. The uppers of the calceus were stitched to a separate sole and might appear in a variety of lengths.

As with other forms of clothing, who wore calcei and what kinds of calcei were worn indicated the social position or status of the wearer. Slaves, for example, were not allowed to wear calcei at all. But statesmen known as senators wore a special kind of calceus that had a high top that covered the ankle. They were secured with four black thongs (leather strips) and a buckle. Emperors wore a different form of calceus, called a mulleus, which was laced with red thongs. Many different varieties of calcei have been discovered in ancient Rome, either from the many statues that survived the era or from actual shoes that have been discovered.

FOR MORE INFORMATION

Kippen, Cameron. *The History of Boots.* http://www.podiatry.curtin.edu. au/boot.html (accessed on July 11, 2003).

Payne, Blanche, Geitel Winakor, and Jane Farrell-Beck. *The History of Costume.* 2nd ed. New York: HarperCollins, 1992.

Yates, James. "Calceus." *Smith's Dictionary: Articles on Clothing and Adornment.* http://www.ukans.edu/history/index/europe/ancient_rome/ E/Roman/Texts/secondary/SMIGRA*/Calceus.html (accessed on July 24, 2003).

Cothurnus

The cothurnus was a distinctive boot typically worn by hunters, horsemen, and men of authority and power in ancient Rome. Made of leather, the boot was pulled on to the foot and laced all the way to the top. It could reach as low as mid calf and as high as the knee. The portion of the boot that covered the lower leg was very close fitting. The boot could be very distinctive, with cut leather patterns adding decoration, or with long laces that were wrapped around the lower leg before they were tied. Like other elements of Roman clothing, the cothurnus became more decorative over time, showing the growing fascination with more elaborate costume.

Originally the soles of the boots were a thin layer of leather, but wearers soon devised ways of padding the sole, often using layers of cork. The padded sole may have been meant to provide protection for the feet, but costume historians suspect that thick layers of cork may have been added to make the wearer appear taller and thus more powerful. Perhaps these were the first "lifts," devices meant to add to someone's height.

The cothurnus also has a long history in theater. In classical Greek and Roman theater the cothurnus was the shoe worn by the players in tragedies, serious plays that showed the conflict between a great man and powerful forces such as destiny or fate. Depending on the importance of the character in the play, the cothurnus was made of different heights. The taller the actor, the more important his role. The cothurnus is still worn in reenactments of classical tragedies, and the word cothurnus has come to stand for the unique style in which such ancient dramas are performed.

FOR MORE INFORMATION

Symons, David J. *Costume of Ancient Rome.* New York: Chelsea House, 1987.

Yates, James. "Cothurnus." *Smith's Dictionary: Articles on Clothing and Adornment.* http://www.ukans.edu/history/index/europe/ancient_rome/E/Roman/Texts/secondary/SMIGRA*/Cothurnus.html (accessed on July 24, 2003).

Crepida

A crepida was a form of footwear that was a cross between a solea, or sandal, and a calceus, or covered shoe. Crepidae, the plural form of crepida, had durable soles and were usually covered on the heel and around the sides, but the tops were open and held together with thongs, leather strips that acted like laces. Romans seem to have borrowed the shoe from their Etruscan neighbors on the Italian peninsula, and it was in wide usage from about 400 B.C.E. to 400 C.E.

At their simplest crepidae were a kind of slipper. Made of a single piece of soft leather that was cut two inches larger than the foot size, it was wrapped up the side of the foot and held in place with a leather thong. This form of the crepida was the common footwear of actors in Roman comedies, chosen because of its simplicity and its usage by common people.

Another form of crepida was worn by citizens of Rome who wanted protection for the soles of their feet. These wooden soled crepidae might have brass or iron tacks nailed into the sole to improve wear. One example of these shoes was actually hinged at the balls of the feet, with the two wooden halves of the shoe fastened with a leather hinge. This hinged shoe made walking easier. Another similar form of crepida was created especially for criminals. This crepida had a thick and heavy wooden sole that was attached to the feet with crude thongs. The heavy shoes were meant to keep a prisoner from escaping.

Though crepidae were generally thought of as common, everyday shoes and were worn by common people, they also could be more highly decorated. One of the interesting things about crepidae is that they were made to fit either foot, instead of specifically fitting a right or a left foot.

FOR MORE INFORMATION

Payne, Blanche, Geitel Winakor, and Jane Farrell-Beck. *The History of Costume.* 2nd ed. New York: HarperCollins, 1992.

Yates, James. "Crepida." *Smith's Dictionary: Articles on Clothing and Adornment.* http://www.ukans.edu/history/index/europe/ancient_rome/E/Roman/Texts/secondary/SMIGRA*/Crepida.html (accessed on July 24, 2003).

Gallicae

Gallicae is a general name given to a style of closed leather boot worn by the men of ancient Rome. The Romans named the boots gallicae because they had first encountered them when they were fighting the northern tribes of Gaul, present-day France, after 100 B.C.E. Roman soldiers on long military campaigns in the cold climate of Gaul adopted the sturdy, protective footwear worn by the natives. When they returned home, these soldiers brought the style back to Rome, where it soon became popular.

During the early years of the Roman Republic, which began around 509 B.C.E., Roman citizens wore very simple footwear. As the Greeks had done before them, both rich and poor Romans mainly went barefoot, especially inside. Outside, they wore simple sandals woven of plant fibers or made of leather. As Roman society developed, and as shoemaking skills increased, shoe styles became more and more elaborate. By the beginning of the Roman Empire in 27 B.C.E., most well-dressed Romans wore stylish solea (sandals), calceus (shoes), and cothurnus (boots), and only the very poor and the slaves went barefoot.

The original gallicae worn by soldiers returning from the wars in Gaul were simple ankle-high boots made from two pieces of leather sewn together in back and laced up the front with leather straps. Roman shoemakers soon developed the Gallic shoe into a rugged tall boot, which was worn by soldiers and farmers for marching, riding, and working in bad weather. During the prosperous years of the empire, when fashion became quite ornate, the simple gallicae evolved into the campagus, a boot worn by the upper classes, such as high-ranking military officers and senators. The campagi were dyed in rich colors, such as red for senators and purple for the emperor. Their height was determined by rank: the higher the boot top, the higher the wearer's position in society. However, gallicae and campagi were not worn with togas, the traditional outer garment worn by Roman citizens.

FOR MORE INFORMATION

Houston, Mary G. *Ancient Greek, Roman, and Byzantine Costume and Decoration.* New York: Barnes and Noble, 1947.

Laver, James. *Costume and Fashion: A Concise History.* 4th ed. New York: Thames and Hudson, 2002.

Solea

The solea, or sandal, was the most common indoor shoe of the ancient Romans. It was a very simple shoe, consisting of a flat sole held to the foot with a simple strap across the instep, similar to today's thongs or flip-flops. Most of the solea known to historians were made of leather. Some, however, were made of wood. Special wooden-soled sandals, called sandalium, were worn by women during the Roman Republic (509–27 B.C.E.) and were later worn by both sexes. It appears that simpler wooden-soled solea were also worn by poorer Romans.

A respectable Roman citizen never wore his or her solea outdoors, just as they never wore their outdoor shoes, or calcei, indoors. When wealthier citizens went to someone else's house or to a public event, they had their servants carry their solea and they changed into them when they arrived at their destination. In fact, the Romans had a saying that related to this custom. To "ask for one's sandals" indicated that one was ready to depart.

There were alternatives to the leather solea. The baxea was very similar to the solea. It had a strap that rose up between the first two toes and was anchored in another strap that crossed the instep of the foot. The baxea were typically made of papyrus leaves or other vegetable fibers that were woven into a durable, thick sole. It is thought that these inexpensive sandals were adopted from the Egyptians, who wore a similar sandal as early as 3100 B.C.E.

FOR MORE INFORMATION

Symons, David J. *Costume of Ancient Rome.* New York: Chelsea House, 1987.

Yates, James. "Solea." *Smith's Dictionary: Articles on Clothing and Adornment.* http://www.ukans.edu/history/index/europe/ancient_rome/E/Roman/ Texts/secondary/SMIGRA*/Solea.html (accessed on July 24, 2003).

[*See also* **Volume 1, Ancient Egypt: Sandals; Volume 1, Ancient Rome: Calceus**]

Where to Learn More

■ ■ ■

The following list of resources focuses on material appropriate for middle school or high school students. Please note that Web site addresses were verified prior to publication but are subject to change.

BOOKS

Batterberry, Michael, and Ariane Batterberry. *Fashion: The Mirror of History.* New York: Greenwich House, 1977.

Bigelow, Marybelle S. *Fashion in History: Apparel in the Western World.* Minneapolis, MN: Burgess Publishing, 1970.

Boucher, François. *20,000 Years of Fashion: The History of Costume and Personal Adornment.* Extended ed. New York: Harry N. Abrams, 1987.

Contini, Mila. *Fashion: From Ancient Egypt to the Present Day.* Edited by James Laver. New York: Odyssey Press, 1965.

Corson, Richard. *Fashions in Hair: The First Five Thousand Years.* London, England: Peter Owen, 2001.

Cosgrave, Bronwyn. *The Complete History of Costume and Fashion: From Ancient Egypt to the Present Day.* New York: Checkmark Books, 2000.

Ewing, Elizabeth; revised and updated by Alice Mackrell. *History of Twentieth Century Fashion.* Lanham, MD: Barnes and Noble Books, 1992.

Hoobler, Dorothy, and Thomas Hoobler. *Vanity Rules: A History of American Fashion and Beauty.* Brookfield, CT: Twenty-First Century Books, 2000.

Laver, James. *Costume and Fashion: A Concise History.* 4th ed. London, England: Thames and Hudson, 2002.

Lawlor, Laurie. *Where Will This Shoe Take You?: A Walk through the History of Footwear.* New York: Walker and Co., 1996.

Lister, Margot. *Costume: An Illustrated Survey from Ancient Times to the Twentieth Century.* London, England: Herbert Jenkins, 1967.

Miller, Brandon Marie. *Dressed for the Occasion: What Americans Wore 1620-1970.* Minneapolis, MN: Lerner Publications, 1999.

Mulvagh, Jane. *Vogue History of 20th Century Fashion.* New York: Viking, 1988.

Payne, Blanche, Geitel Winakor, and Jane Farrell-Beck. *The History of Costume.* 2nd ed. New York: HarperCollins, 1992.

Peacock, John. *The Chronicle of Western Fashion: From Ancient Times to the Present Day.* New York: Harry N. Abrams, 1991.

Perl, Lila. *From Top Hats to Baseball Caps, from Bustles to Blue Jeans: Why We Dress the Way We Do.* New York: Clarion Books, 1990.

Pratt, Lucy, and Linda Woolley. *Shoes.* London, England: V&A Publications, 1999.

Racinet, Auguste. *The Historical Encyclopedia of Costumes.* New York: Facts on File, 1988.

Ribeiro, Aileen. *The Gallery of Fashion.* Princeton, NJ: Princeton University Press, 2000.

Rowland-Warne, L. *Costume.* New York: Dorling Kindersley, 2000.

Schnurnberger, Lynn Edelman. *Let There Be Clothes: 40,000 Years of Fashion.* New York: Workman, 1991.

Schoeffler, O. E., and William Gale. *Esquire's Encyclopedia of 20th Century Men's Fashions.* New York: McGraw-Hill, 1973.

Sichel, Marion. *History of Men's Costume.* New York: Chelsea House, 1984.

Steele, Valerie. *Fifty Years of Fashion: New Look to Now.* New Haven, CT: Yale University Press, 1997.

Trasko, Mary. *Daring Do's: A History of Extraordinary Hair.* New York: Flammarion, 1994.

Yarwood, Doreen. *The Encyclopedia of World Costume.* New York: Charles Scribner's Sons, 1978.

Yarwood, Doreen. *Fashion in the Western World, 1500–1990.* New York: Drama Book Publishers, 1992.

WEB SITES

Bender, A. *La Couturière Parisienne.* http://marquise.de/index.html (accessed on September 10, 2003).

Kathie Rothkop Hair Design. *Hair History.* http://www.hairrific.com/hist.htm (accessed on September 10, 2003).

Ladnier, Penny D. Dunlap. *The Costume Gallery.* http://www.costume gallery.com (accessed on September 10, 2003).

Maginnis, Tara. *The Costumer's Manifesto.* http://www.costumes.org/ (accessed on September 10, 2003).

Metropolitan Museum of Art. *The Costume Institute.* http://www. metmuseum.org/collections/department.asp?dep=8 (accessed on September 10, 2003).

Museum of Costume, Bath. http://www.museumofcostume.co.uk (accessed on September 10, 2003).

Sardo, Julie Zetterberg. *The Costume Page: Costuming Resources Online.* http://members.aol.com/nebula5/costume.html (accessed on September 10, 2003).

Thomas, Pauline Weston, and Guy Thomas. *Fashion-Era.* http://www. fashion-era.com/index.htm (accessed on September 10, 2003).

Index

■ ■ ■

Italic type indicates volume number; **boldface** type indicates main entries and then page numbers; (ill.) indicates photos and illustrations.

B

C

D

▌▌ G

H

K

M

X

Y

Z